Accelerated Reader
Reading level: 9.4
Point value: 5.0
Test number: 103716

The Early
Middle Ages

Other titles in the World History Series

WORLD HISTORY

The Early Middle Ages

James A. Corrick

LUCENT BOOKS

An imprint of Thomson Gale, a part of The Thomson Corporation

THOMSON

GALE

Detroit • New York • San Francisco • San Diego • New Haven, Conn. • Waterville, Maine • London • Munich

LIBRARY OF CONGRESS CATALOGING-IN-PUBLICATION DATA

Corrick, James A.
  The early Middle Ages / by James A. Corrick.
    p. cm. — (World history)
  Originally published: San Diego, CA : Lucent Books, 1995.
  Includes bibliographical references and index.
  ISBN 1-59018-652-4 (alk. paper)
    1. Europe—History—476–1492—Juvenile literature. 2. Civilization, Medieval—Juvenile literature. I. Title. II. Series: World history series.
D121.C67 2005
909.07—dc22
                                                                                2005012374

Printed in the United States of America

Contents

Foreword

Each year, on the first day of school, nearly every history teacher faces the task of explaining why his or her students should study history. Many reasons have been given. One is that lessons exist in the past from which contemporary society can benefit and learn. Another is that exploration of the past allows us to see the origins of our customs, ideas, and institutions. Concepts such as democracy, ethnic conflict, or even things as trivial as fashion or mores, have historical roots.

Reasons such as these impress few students, however. If anything, these explanations seem remote and dull to young minds. Yet history is anything but dull. And therein lies what is perhaps the most compelling reason for studying history: History is filled with great stories. The classic themes of literature and drama—love and sacrifice, hatred and revenge, injustice and betrayal, adversity and overcoming adversity—fill the pages of history books, feeding the imagination as well as any of the great works of fiction do.

The story of the Children's Crusade, for example, is one of the most tragic in history. In 1212 Crusader fever hit Europe. A call went out from the pope that all good Christians should journey to Jerusalem to drive out the hated Muslims and return the city to Christian control. Heeding the call, thousands of children made the jour-

ney. Parents bravely allowed many children to go, and entire communities were inspired by the faith of these small Crusaders. Unfortunately, many boarded ships captained by slave traders, who enthusiastically sold the children into slavery as soon as they arrived at their destination. Thousands died from disease, exposure, and starvation on the long march across Europe to the Mediterranean Sea. Others perished at sea.

Another story, from a modern and more familiar place, offers a soul-wrenching view of personal humiliation but also the ability to rise above it. Hatsuye Egami was one of 110,000 Japanese Americans sent to internment camps during World War II. "Since yesterday we Japanese have ceased to be human beings," he wrote in his diary. "We are numbers. We are no longer Egamis, but the number 23324. A tag with that number is on every trunk, suitcase and bag. Tags, also, on our breasts." Despite such dehumanizing treatment, most internees worked hard to control their bitterness. They created workable communities inside the camps and demonstrated again and again their loyalty as Americans.

These are but two of the many stories from history that can be found in the pages of the Lucent Books World History series. All World History titles rely on sound research and verifiable evidence, and all give students a clear sense of time, place, and chronology through maps and timelines as well as text.

All titles include a wide range of authoritative perspectives that demonstrate the complexity of historical interpretation and sharpen the reader's critical thinking skills. Formally documented quotations and annotated bibliographies enable students to locate and evaluate sources, often instantaneously via the Internet, and serve as valuable tools for further research and debate.

Finally, Lucent's World History titles present rousing good stories, featuring vivid primary source quotations drawn from unique, sometimes obscure sources such as diaries, public records, and contemporary chronicles. In this way, the voices of participants and witnesses as well as important biographers and historians bring the study of history to life. As we are caught up in the lives of others, we are reminded that we too are characters in the ongoing human saga, and we are better prepared for our own roles.

Important Dates During

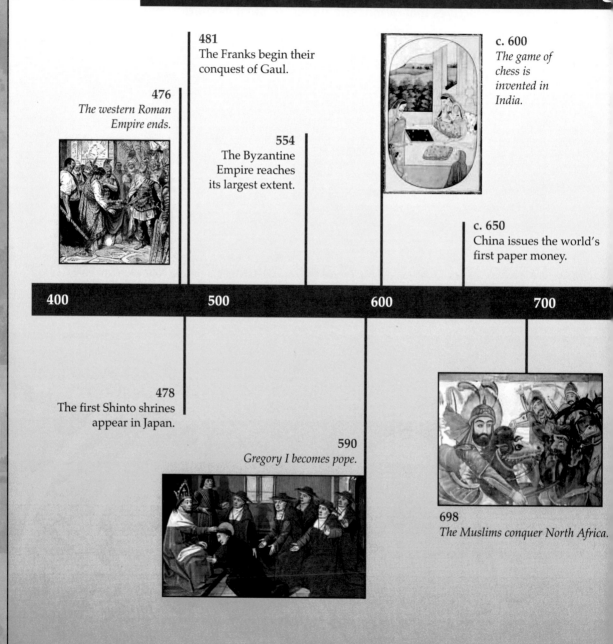

476
The western Roman Empire ends.

481
The Franks begin their conquest of Gaul.

554
The Byzantine Empire reaches its largest extent.

c. 600
The game of chess is invented in India.

c. 650
China issues the world's first paper money.

400   500   600   700

478
The first Shinto shrines appear in Japan.

590
Gregory I becomes pope.

698
The Muslims conquer North Africa.

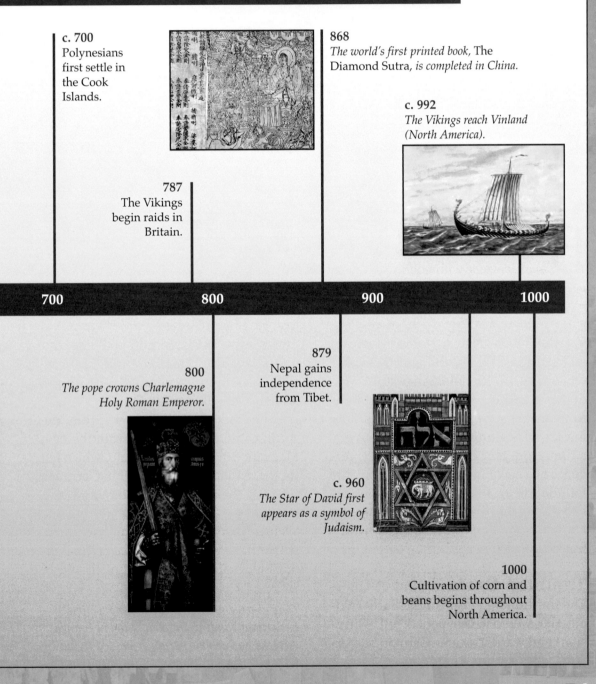

c. 700
Polynesians first settle in the Cook Islands.

868
The world's first printed book, The Diamond Sutra, *is completed in China.*

c. 992
The Vikings reach Vinland (North America).

787
The Vikings begin raids in Britain.

700   800   900   1000

879
Nepal gains independence from Tibet.

800
The pope crowns Charlemagne Holy Roman Emperor.

c. 960
The Star of David first appears as a symbol of Judaism.

1000
Cultivation of corn and beans begins throughout North America.

The Beginnings of a New Civilization

By the fifth century A.D. the Roman Empire, which had provided its many citizens with political and economic stability for centuries, was crumbling. It suffered both from internal problems, most notably a corrupt and inefficient government, and from repeated invasions. In 476 the empire ended when Emperor Romulus Augustulus was deposed and the first in a series of non-Roman kings took his place. This date marks the beginning of the Middle Ages, a thousand-year era that saw the emergence of a new European civilization. The foundation for that new civilization was laid during the period's first five centuries, known as the Early Middle Ages, which lasted until 1000.

Troubled Times

The five hundred years of the Early Middle Ages were a violent period, full of invasions and war. First came German barbarians, who set up kingdoms in former Roman lands in the west. The Franks occupied Gaul; the Visigoths conquered Spain; and the Angles, Saxons, and Jutes invaded Britain. Even Italy, the heartland of the old Roman Empire, was in part taken over, first by the Ostrogoths and then by the Lombards. The Roman Empire survived only in Greece, Asia Minor, the Middle East, and Egypt, eventually becoming known as the Byzantine Empire.

Other invaders followed. From the south came Muslims and from the east Magyars. Still, except for Spain, which fell to the Muslims in 714, the Germans retained their hold on western and central Europe. Then, from the north came Vikings, themselves Germanic tribesmen, whose raids terrified Europeans throughout the final two centuries of the Early

This nineteenth-century painting depicts barbarians landing in what is today France. Attacks by such barbarian tribes led to the fall of the Roman Empire in the fifth century.

Middle Ages before they finally ceased in the late 900s. With the end of the Viking era came an end to the waves of invaders and the social chaos that they often left in their wake.

The Dark Ages

The turmoil of the Early Middle Ages colored the way the period—indeed, the entire Middle Ages—was viewed by those who came immediately after. During the Renaissance, scholars invented the term *Middle Ages* because they viewed the sixth through the fifteenth centuries as literally a middle period in the history of the world. To these scholars the Middle Ages were sandwiched between Greek and Roman civilization and the Renaissance.

Renaissance historians also saw the Middle Ages as a backward time, in which learning disappeared and progress of all sorts stopped. For them the worst of the period was the Early Middle Ages because of the social chaos that followed the fall of

Rome and because of the rapid loss of much Greek and Roman culture. They called this five-hundred-year period the Dark Ages. As a result of these attitudes, they believed that Renaissance Europe was the direct heir of ancient Greece and Rome and owed nothing to the medieval period. This view still exists today, as historian C. Warren Hollister points out: "The Middle Ages . . . [are] still viewed by some as a long, stupid

An eleventh-century manuscript page depicts a bishop blessing a monk. The Christian church was an important institution during the Early Middle Ages because it had the strength to stand up to barbarism.

detour in the march of human progress—a thousand years of poverty, superstition, and gloom that divided the old golden age of the Roman Empire from the new golden age of the . . . Renaissance."[1]

The Modern View

Most modern scholars, however, view the Middle Ages more favorably. For them the era was no more backward than the classical world of Greece and Rome, and its civilization was not inferior to that of the ancient world. Indeed, one reason that the Middle Ages are important is that they did create a civilization that is the direct ancestor of modern western culture. According to the scholar M. Paul Viollet, "what we are, we are in large measure because of the Middle Ages. The Middle Ages live in us; they are alive all around us."[2]

Further, even though present-day historians still call this era the Middle Ages, they now recognize that these thousand years were not a middle period in the history of the world or even of Europe. To modern scholars the Middle Ages are just another episode in the ongoing story of western civilization that stretches from ancient Greece to the present.

Innovations

As they do the Middle Ages in general, most present-day historians also view the Early Middle Ages in a more positive light than did Renaissance scholars. Modern medievalists agree with the historian Justine Davis Randers-Pehrson that the period was "essentially a time of adjustment and beginnings."[3]

In this process of adjustment, the inhabitants of the Early Middle Ages created many new ways of organizing society to replace those lost with the disappearance of the Roman Empire. Thus, for example, in the Early Middle Ages feudalism was born. In this political setup, which reached its peak in the Late Middle Ages, one aristocrat promised service, particularly military assistance, to another in exchange for certain rights, such as the use of large farming estates.

These farming estates, known as manors, became the basic unit of medieval society. Here, generations of people lived and worked, with most of their essential needs supplied by the crops and livestock they raised. Except for the aristocrats who had military and political duties elsewhere, the residents of a manor had little reason to leave it.

These social innovations were also accompanied by technical inventiveness that produced more food more efficiently. One of the most important of these inventions was a new kind of collar that allowed a horse to pull a plow without being choked. Thus, the new collar let horses plow more land than in premedieval times, resulting in larger harvests. This increased food production, in turn, paved the way for the population explosion of the Late Middle Ages and the Renaissance.

Shifting Civilization

In addition to introducing social and technical innovations, the Early Middle Ages are important because during this period European civilization moved away from the Mediterranean Sea. Until the fifth century A.D. European civilization meant Mediterranean civilization because Europe's first

The Early Middle Ages gave rise to feudalism in Europe. Under this political system, peasants worked the land held by a lord in exchange for protection from invading armies.

two great cultures, Greek and Roman, were located on the shores of that sea. However, by 1000 the center of European civilization had shifted north. Here, kingdoms existed that during the Late Middle Ages became nations, such as England and France.

In general, then, the foundation of the Late Middle Ages and, as a consequence, the modern western world was laid in the Early Middle Ages. Historian Archibald R. Lewis writes that because "the Early Mid-

dle Ages . . . were the seedbed out of which our modern Western world emerged, to understand them is to grasp the richness of our own special heritage."[4]

Among the most important players on the Early Middle Ages stage were the German barbarians. The Germans had been held in check by the Roman Empire until the beginning of the fifth century A.D. Then they overran the crumbling remains of the empire, taking control of much of it and the rest of western and northern Europe. During the centuries of the Early Middle Ages, the Germans superimposed their culture on the remains of Greek and Roman civilization, producing the beginnings of medieval civilization.

Chapter One

The Barbarians

By tradition, historians mark the end of the ancient world and the beginning of the Early Middle Ages with the overthrow of the Emperor Romulus Augustulus in 476. In reality, the fall of Rome was not a single event. Even before 476 the Roman Empire had lost territory to invading German tribes, who had set up kingdoms in former Roman lands. As historian David Nicholas notes, "the Roman Empire . . . evolved gradually into the Europe of the Germanic . . . kingdoms."[5]

The Germans

To the Romans, the Germans were barbarians, which was not the insult that it is today. Romans considered anyone who did not speak Latin or Greek to be a barbarian.

Until the first century A.D. the Germans were a group of tribes living in what is now Denmark, northern Poland, and northern Germany. Each tribe was made up of several extended families, each claiming descent from a common ances-

tor. These family groups lived in small villages, often with houses built around a central point from which extended fields of barley, wheat, oats, and rye.

At the top of German society was the warrior, who either inherited his rank or earned it in battle. Below the warrior were men unable to fight, women, children, and slaves.

Few German tribes were headed by a single chief. Instead, most practiced a rough form of democracy. A council made up of the senior men from each family made day-to-day decisions, but anything important, such as going to war, had to be voted on by all the tribe's warriors. The first-century A.D. Roman historian Tacitus writes:

> Concerning minor matters the chiefs deliberate, but in important affairs all the . . . [warriors] are consulted, although the subjects referred to the common people for judgment are discussed beforehand by the chiefs. Unless some sudden and unexpected

event calls them together they assemble on fixed days. . . . When the crowd is sufficient they take their place fully armed. . . . Then the king or a chief addresses them [the assembled warriors]. . . . If an opinion is displeasing they reject it by shouting; if they agree to it they clash with their spears.[6]

Contact with Rome

One of the matters that required input from a tribe's warriors was migration, which by the first century A.D. was becoming increasingly common. Behind these migrations was a growing population that forced some Germanic tribes to move south in the hopes of finding more living space.

The migrating barbarians quickly ran up against the northern borders of the Roman Empire, marked by the Rhine and Danube rivers. They were no match for the better armed and better trained Roman soldiers. Thus, the Germans were generally unsuccessful in forcing their way across these rivers and into the empire itself.

This illustration depicts the leader of a Germanic tribe. Warriors were at the top of the social hierarchy in such tribes.

This seventh-century carving depicts the army of a Germanic tribe known as the Lombards.

Still, the Germans found that they could enter Roman lands as single individuals and small family groups. So many of them drifted across the borders, becoming farm workers and soldiers. German and Roman traders also crossed the border. Thus, by 400 the line dividing the German and Roman worlds was no longer sharp. Germans were scattered all through the empire, and the Roman army had many Germans serving in it, with Germans even rising to become Roman generals.

A Weakened Empire

For almost three hundred years the Romans kept the Germans from successfully invading the empire. However, in the last decades of the fourth century the borders gave way, and barbarian army after army marched into the empire.

These invasions succeeded for several reasons. First, Germans who had traded and soldiered in the empire spread detailed reports about imperial defenses, troop positions, and tactics to their fellows outside the empire.

Second, Rome was no longer a united state and did not present a united front to the barbarians. Because the empire had proven too large to rule from the city of Rome, the Romans had divided their empire into western and eastern sections. Each section had its own emperor, and the two wielded equal power. In general, each imperial section was responsible for its own security, with troops from the west rarely serving in the east and vice versa.

Third, the armies in both western and eastern empires were understaffed, with neither having enough soldiers to protect the long imperial borders. The shortage of soldiers was the consequence of a population decline caused by a series of plagues in the third and fourth centuries. Even with the addition of mercenaries, troop levels were below what was needed.

Finally, Roman leadership during this period was generally poor. In both the western and eastern sections weak and incompetent emperors ruled, and imperial officials frequently diverted money meant for the army into their own purses. Additionally, when strong leaders did appear they were assassinated by political rivals who feared their growing power.

The Visigoths

The first important Germanic invaders to take advantage of Rome's weaknesses were the Visigoths. Around 376 the Visigoths

---

Living Among the Barbarians

In An Embassy to the Huns, *quoted in* Medieval Europe, *edited by C. Warren Hollister, the fifth-century Roman trader Priscus writes of a fellow Roman living among the barbarian Scythians (Huns).*

He considered his new life among the Scythians better than his old life among the Romans, and the reasons he urged were as follows: "After war the Scythians live at leisure, enjoying what they have got. . . . The Romans, on the other hand, are . . . very liable to be killed, if there are any hostilities, since they have to rest their hopes of protection on others [professional soldiers]. . . .

"But the condition of Roman subjects in time of peace is far more grievous than the evils of war, for the exaction of . . . taxes is very severe, and unprincipled men inflict injuries on others because the laws are . . . not valid against all classes [of society]. A transgressor who belongs to the wealthy classes is not punished for his injustice, while a poor man . . . undergoes the legal penalty. . . . The climax of misery is to have to pay in order to obtain justice. For no one will give a hearing to the injured man except he pay . . . money to the judge and the judge's clerks."

were driven from their homes in Romania by the Huns, a nomadic people who invaded Europe from central Asia. The Germans pushed south across the Danube and into the eastern empire. In 378, after defeating an eastern imperial army at Adrianople, the Visigoths struck a deal with the Romans, who allowed them to settle on land just south of the Danube. The Romans also promised to pay the Visigoths an annual tribute in gold.

Peace lasted for a generation until the eastern empire, deciding that it had paid enough tribute, stopped its gold payments. In 402, angered by this Roman defiance, the war chieftain Alaric led the Visigoths on raids deep into the eastern empire and then, turning west, invaded Italy. In 410,

after two unsuccessful attempts, the Visigoths captured Rome, which they looted for three days. From Rome the Germans turned north, this time invading the Roman province of Gaul, roughly equal to present-day France. Rome worked out another deal with the barbarians that gave them a region in southern Gaul as a separate Gothic kingdom. Beginning in 466, the Visigoths pushed their kingdom farther south, taking over Spain from the Romans.

The Visigothic kingdom was only the first of many German domains carved out of the western Roman Empire. As the scholar Crane Brinton observes, "the Visigoths were pioneers, signs of what was to come. They gained the first spectacular field victories over the Romans, and their

Led by the war chief Alaric, the Visigoths invaded and sacked Rome in 410. Eventually the Visigoths created their own kingdom out of pieces of the former western Roman Empire.

A Barbarian Victory

In 378 the Visigoths defeated an eastern Roman army at Adrianople. The following eyewitness account by Ammianus Marcellinus is found in A Source Book of Medieval History, *edited by Frederic Austin Ogg.*

Our men came in sight of the wagons of the enemy, which . . . [were] arranged in a circle. According to their custom, the barbarian host [army] raised a fierce and hideous yell, while the Roman generals marshalled their line of battle. . . .

And . . . arms and missiles of all kinds were meeting in fierce conflict, . . . terrifying our soldiers, numbers of whom were pierced by strokes of the javelins hurled at them, and by arrows.

Then the two lines of battle dashed against each other. . . . Our left wing had advanced . . . but they were deserted by the rest of the cavalry, and . . . they were . . . beaten down. . . . Presently, our infantry also was left unsupported. . . . And by this time such clouds of dust arose that it was scarcely possible to see the sky, which resounded with terrible cries. . . . The barbarians . . . beat down our horses and men and left no spot to which our ranks could fall back to operate. . . .

Amid all this great . . . confusion our infantry were exhausted by toil and danger, until at last they had neither the strength left to fight nor spirit to plan anything. . . . The sun . . . scorched the Romans. . . . At last our columns were entirely beaten back. . . . Scarcely one third of the whole army escaped.

kingdom . . . was the precedent [model] for a whole . . . series of barbarian 'concessions.'"[7] These concessions meant that the Roman west lost control of large sections of its empire. As the west conceded southern Gaul and Spain to the Visigoths, it would later concede more land to other German tribes until little was left but Italy. Many of these concessions would form the kingdoms of the Middle Ages.

The Vandals

In addition to the land they took directly from the Roman west, the Visigoths also enabled other invaders to move into the western empire. Constant Visigothic attacks forced the Romans to pull troops away from the borders. So, while Alaric and his Goths marched into Italy, other Germans charged across the Rhine and looted and burned their way down through Gaul.

Most barbarians grabbed imperial land in this province and held onto it. However, one group, the Vandals, continued onward into the portion of North Africa controlled by the western empire. Here, the Vandals overthrew Roman rule.

The loss of North Africa was a serious blow to the western Romans. First, it was a rich province, and its loss sapped the west's ability to pay and equip its soldiers, let alone maintain the roads the army depended upon to reach its enemies quickly. Second, it was an ideal base from which the Vandals could launch naval raids against Italy, particularly Rome. In 455 the Vandals captured the city, which they looted before returning to their North African kingdom.

Attila and the Huns

Not all the invaders of the Roman Empire were German. Indeed, the most feared barbarians were the non-German Huns. These nomads were excellent horsemen who inspired fear with their ferocious charges and unpredictable but winning battle tactics. Their battle savvy won them control of the land that stretched from the Caspian Sea to the Alps, an area almost as large as the entire Roman Empire.

In 434 the Huns came under the rule of a new king, Attila. According to the sixth-century German writer Jordanes, Attila was imposing.

He was a man born into the world to shake the nations, the scourge of all the lands, who in some way terrified all mankind by the rumors . . . concerning him. He was haughty in his walk . . . so that the power of his proud

This nineteenth-century illustration depicts the Vandals' attack on Rome in 455. These Germanic invaders sacked the Roman Empire's capital and departed with their plunder.

spirit appeared in the movement of his body. He was indeed a lover of war, yet restrained in action; mighty in counsel . . . lenient to those who were received under his protection.[8]

In 451, after a series of successful campaigns against the eastern empire that brought the Huns much gold and other loot, Attila turned his attention to the weaker west. However, the west proved stronger than it appeared. Invading Gaul, Attila suffered his only defeat, being beaten by a combined Roman and Visigothic army.

The Hun leader quickly regrouped and in 452 entered Italy. Although the Huns looted several Italian cities, they failed to reach Rome. Tradition has it that Pope Leo the Great talked Attila out of plundering the city. In reality, a plague and famine sweeping Italy at the time saved Rome. Afraid of the disease and unable to feed themselves in the famine-gripped land, the Huns retreated before they reached Rome.

Not long after this retreat, Attila died. The Hun empire was then divided among his many sons, who quarreled and fought over their shares of it. Various conquered peoples, seizing their chance, revolted. The breakup of the Huns' empire ended their threat to both the old Roman Empire and the new Germanic kingdoms. Still, Attila's failed invasion caused much destruction and loss of life, further draining the resources of the western empire and contributing to its eventual fall.

A Shattered Empire

In the decades after the Hun invasion, important changes took place in the Roman

The fearsome Attila, leader of the Huns, led an invasion of Italy in 452, looting several cities but ultimately sparing Rome.

with the permission of the eastern emperor, Odoacer ruled as an imperial governor over the west.

The eastern empire was still intact, its smaller area making it more easily defended and governed. In theory the eastern emperor was now sole ruler of both sections of the Roman Empire. In practice, however, he had limited authority in the west. In recognition of this limited influence, modern historians prefer to view the post-476 eastern empire as a new state, which they call the Byzantine Empire.

Theodoric the Great

Under Odoacer life in the remains of the western empire continued much as it always had. Over time, however, Odoacer became more powerful and, consequently, increasingly more independent of eastern control. Finally, the Byzantine emperor Zeno decided to remove him. In 493 he offered rule of the west to another group of Germans, the Ostrogoths. Under the leadership of the chieftain Theodoric, the Ostrogoths invaded Italy, capturing and killing Odoacer.

Empire. In the west the empire lost almost all its territory except for Italy and parts of Gaul. Additionally, a non-Roman, the barbarian Odoacer, was now ruler. Although the barbarian had deposed the western Roman emperor Romulus Augustulus, he had not tried to become emperor himself. Instead,

Like Odoacer, Theodoric, now known as the Great, kept the west culturally Roman. He even tried to reform the government by combating the widespread corruption of the Roman civil service. He launched an ambitious program that cleaned up harbors, repaired aqueducts, and restored churches and public buildings. Like most Germans, Theodoric admired the old empire and its accomplishments, as he made clear in the following public letter:

> We [Theodoric] delight to live after the law of the Romans, whom we seek to defend . . . and we are as much interested in the maintenance of morality as we can possibly be in war. For what profit is there in having removed the turmoil of the Barbarians unless we live according to law? . . . Let other kings desire the glory of battles won, of cities taken, of ruins made; our purpose is . . . so to rule that our subjects shall grieve that they did not earlier acquire the blessing of our dominion.[9]

This illustration shows the barbarian Odoacer forcing the western Roman emperor Romulus Augustulus to give up his throne in 476. Odoacer then became imperial governor of the western empire.

Although Theodoric, along with many he ruled, saw himself as a Roman leader, the Ostrogoths as a whole remained outsiders to Roman society. Indeed, Theodoric encouraged this separation between the Goths and the Romans. He was afraid that if his German followers became civilized, they would become soft and no longer be the warriors he needed to keep Italy secure from other invaders.

The Struggle for Power

Upon Theodoric's death in 526, his nine-year-old grandson Athalaric became king. However, since the boy was too young to govern, his mother—Theodoric's daughter, Amalasuntha—was the actual ruler. Although intelligent, capable, and well educated, Amalasuntha was unable to win over the Gothic aristocrats. They resented taking orders from a woman, and they further disliked Amalasuntha's giving her son a Roman education.

Still, Amalasuntha managed to hold onto power because it was Athalaric, not she, who was supposedly the ruler. Additionally, she strengthened her position by allying herself with the Byzantine emperor. And finally, when all else failed, she had her enemies killed.

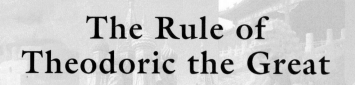

The Rule of Theodoric the Great

The following passage from the letters of Cassiodorus, secretary to Theodoric the Great, is reprinted in The Middle Ages, *edited by Brian Tierney, and illustrates the Ostrogothic ruler's intense interest in the welfare of the people he governed.*

If the people of Rome will beautify their City we will help them. . . . Let nothing lie useless which may redound to [have a good effect upon] the beauty of the City. . . . Cause the blocks of marble which are everywhere lying about in ruins to be wrought into walls. . . . Only take care to use only those stones which have really fallen from public buildings, as we do not wish to appropriate private property, even for the glorification of the City. . . .

It should be only the surplus of the crops of any Province, beyond what is needed for the supply of its own wants, that should be exported. Station persons in the harbours to see that foreign ships do not take away produce to foreign shores until the Public Providers have got all that they require. . . .

Impress upon all . . . subordinates that we would rather that our Treasury lost a [law] suit [brought by the government against a supposed delinquent taxpayer] than that it gained one wrongfully, rather that we lost money than that the taxpayer was driven to suicide. . . . We cannot command the religion of our subjects, since no one can be forced to believe against his will.

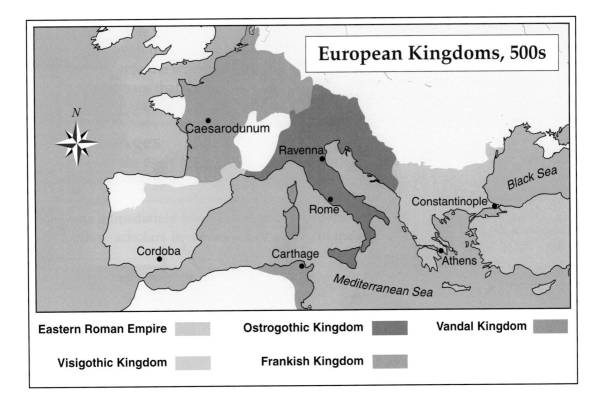

European Kingdoms, 500s

Caesarodunum
Ravenna
Rome
Cordoba
Carthage
Constantinople
Athens
Black Sea
Mediterranean Sea

Eastern Roman Empire **Ostrogothic Kingdom** **Vandal Kingdom**

Visigothic Kingdom **Frankish Kingdom**

At sixteen Athalaric died, and Amalasuntha found that the Goths no longer followed her orders. She, therefore, made a bargain with her cousin, Theodehad. The latter was to have the title of king, but Amalasuntha was to be the actual ruler. However, as soon as Theodehad became king, he had her thrown into prison, where she was strangled by her political enemies.

The Final Blow

The Byzantine emperor Justinian saw this murder as an excuse for retaking the west from the Goths. For some years he had wanted to rebuild the old empire, and a necessary first step was for Italy to be under his direct rule.

Thus, in 535, Justinian sent an army to Italy. The Byzantine troops quickly took much of Italy, but then Gothic resistance grew stronger. For almost twenty years the two sides fought a long string of battles that raged up and down the Italian peninsula. Finally, in 552 the Goths were driven from Italy, leaving the Byzantine Empire in control.

However, after almost two decades of war, the western Roman Empire was completely gone. The city of Rome was devastated more thoroughly by this war than by all the previous German raids combined. The few remaining sections of the western empire easily broke away from imperial control, and the Byzantine Empire had no resources left with which to reconquer them. The Early Middle Ages was fully under way. Only one institution, the Christian church, remained intact to provide some semblance of unity to western Europe.

Chapter Two

The Church

By the sixth century only one organ-ization remained that could provide direction to western Europe: the Christian church. The church survived because, according to historian Norman F. Cantor, it had "two . . . institutions that alone had the strength and efficiency to withstand . . . the surrounding barbarism: the regular clergy (that is monks) and the papacy."[10] The latter would provide the church with leadership, while the former would be crucial to the development of Early Middle Ages civilization.

Church Hierarchy

The Christian church had been the state religion of Rome since 382. The emper-or was the head of the church as he was of the empire. Below the emperor was the clergy—priests and bishops. Priests made up the largest part of the clergy, with each priest being in charge of a church. A bishop was an administrator, a priest who was in charge of a large area, known as a bishopric, that con-tained several churches.

In theory, after the breakup of the Roman Empire, the Byzantine emperor, the heir to Rome, remained leader of the church in both the east and the west. And, indeed, he did rule the church in the east. In the west, however, the emperor's authority was almost nonexistent since Byzantine control was limited to Italy and southern Spain. Most of the west was com-pletely outside the imperial reach.

The Pope

For the first few decades of the Early Middle Ages, the western church had no effective central leadership. For the most part, bishops ran their bishoprics as they saw fit. Nevertheless, the bishop of Rome, known as the pope, did claim to be the head of the western church. His claim rested on his location in Rome, which even after the western empire's collapse was seen as a center of power.

Additionally, Rome had been the city from which secular court decisions had come, so it was logical for the bishop of Rome to settle the tricky issues of Christianity; this role gave him a dominant voice in the church. Finally, since by tradition Christ's disciple Peter brought the Christian church to Rome, the pope was seen as Peter—and thus Christ's—spiritual descendant.

Despite these arguments, the pope's authority was almost as limited as the Byzantine emperor's because he had no way to enforce orders to clergy outside of Italy. He could only hope that as bishop of Rome his dictates would be followed.

Gregory the Great

Then, in 590, Gregory I, also known as Gregory the Great, became pope and immediately set out to broaden the papacy's powers. Gregory realized that the church was in danger of falling apart without some sort of strong central authority. The scholar Ralph H.C. Davis observes that "it was no longer sufficient for the Papacy to claim the 'primacy' of the Church. It had to govern it, and to control even the remotest parts . . . by its own central authority."[11]

In all that the new pope planned, however, he had to tread cautiously so as not to appear to challenge the Byzantine emperor as head of the entire church. The Byzantines had troops stationed in Italy who could easily march to Rome and remove a troublesome pope. Gregory was thus careful to acknowledge the emperor's leadership before embarking on his program.

In Rome, the pope was considered to be a spiritual descendant of Christ but he exercised little control over clergy outside of Italy.

This fourteenth-century illustration features a fanciful depiction of the plague descending on a European city (top) and a more realistic picture of the election of Pope Gregory I in 590.

The Pope Instructs

In 590 Pope Gregory I wrote The Book of the Pastoral Rule, *reprinted here from* A Source Book of Medieval History, *edited by Frederic Austin Ogg. Gregory explains how he expected priests and bishops to perform their duties.*

The ruler [the priest] should always be pure in thought . . . for the hand that would cleanse dirt must needs be clean, lest . . . it soil all the more whatever it touches.

The ruler should always be a leader in action, that by his living he may point out the way of life to those who are put under him . . . and that . . . [those under him] may learn how to walk rather through example than through words. . . .

The ruler ought also to understand how commonly vices pass themselves off as virtues. . . .

Let us now set forth after what manner he should teach. For, . . . one and the same exhortation [instruction] does not suit all . . . [because] all are not bound together by similarity of character. For the things that profit some often hurt others. . . . Therefore, . . . the discourse of teachers . . . [should] be fashioned . . . to suit all and each for their several needs, and yet never deviate the art of common edification.

In 590 Pope Gregory I set down specific rules dictating how priests and bishops should carry out their religious responsibilities.

The Pope and the Clergy

In order to achieve his goals, Gregory had to gain control of the western clergy. As it was, because many bishops were appointed by local rulers to whom they were often related, their first loyalty was to these rulers, not to the church. To counter this problem, Gregory began to fill church posts with his own appointees. Later popes would continue this practice, with the result that papal appointees tended to be more loyal and more obedient to the

This image from a 1402 tapestry depicts Christian missionaries preaching to a pagan audience.

pope than those who had come to office independently of him.

In addition, Gregory insisted that the clergy take a vow of celibacy, that is, that priests neither marry nor engage in sex. This ban was to keep priests from handing church offices down to their children and thus filling up slots that could otherwise be filled by papal appointees.

Arian Christians

Gregory also found other ways to extend the authority of the papacy. First, he brought the Visigoths and another group of Germans, the Lombards, who had conquered northern Italy in 572, into the Church of Rome. Both Goths and Lombards were Christians, but their brand of Christianity, Arianism, differed from that of Rome. Where the Roman church believed that God, Christ, and the Holy Ghost were equal parts of a single being, the Trinity, the Arian church thought that God, because he had fathered Jesus, was superior to his son.

Gregory sent representatives to the Visigoths and Lombards who persuaded the German leaders to become members of the Church of Rome. The conversions had little to do with religious conviction and much to do with political reality. Both the Visigoths and the Lombards had conquered people who had been members of the Church of Rome for centuries. These conquered populations resented the Germans for what was perceived as their mistaken version of Christianity. By converting, the Germans made themselves more acceptable to their subjects. The papacy profited because the loyalty of these new converts was to Rome and to the pope.

Mission to Britain

There were still many Germans who had not embraced Christianity, however, and Gregory saw another opportunity to increase papal power by bringing them into the church. Thus, he sent a mission to Britain, which was now ruled by the pagan Angles, Jutes, and Saxons.

Gregory assumed direct papal control of the mission to Britain. Historian Ralph H.C. Davis explains that Augustine, the man Gregory sent, "had the virtue of obedience. He obeyed the instructions that the Pope had given him, and, when confronted with unforseen difficulties, wrote back to Rome for further advice. . . . The conversion of the English was therefore Gregory's own achievement."[12] As converts of the papacy, Christians in Britain thus looked directly to Rome for guidance.

The Reasons for Missionary Success

Many more missionaries would go out over the next centuries to pull other parts of non-Christian Europe into the church and place them under the direction of the pope. These missionaries succeeded because they studied the society they sought to convert, generally learning the language in order to speak directly to the people without a translator.

Whenever possible, the missionaries worked references to local customs into their teachings. With the Germans, for instance, the missionaries appealed to their warrior ways. Historian David Nicholas writes that "the missionaries were careful to emphasize the heroic deeds of Old Testament figures in preaching to the Germans.

Missionaries in Britain

In The Ecclesiastical History of the English People, *quoted in* A Source Book of Medieval History, *edited by Frederic Austin Ogg, the eighth-century Benedictine monk Bede describes missionary work in Britain.*

The powerful Ethelbert was at that time king of Kent [a region in southeast England]. . . . When Augustine [the head missionary] . . . had preached to him, . . . the king answered thus: "Your words . . . are very fair, but as they are new to us, and of uncertain import, I cannot . . . forsake that which I have so long followed. . . . But . . . we will not . . . forbid you to preach and win as many as you can to your religion.' . . .

As soon as they [the missionaries] entered the dwelling place assigned them, they began . . . living . . . in conformity with what they prescribed for others. . . . There was . . . a church . . . built whilst the Romans were still in the island, . . . [in which] they first began to . . . preach, and to baptize, until the king being converted to the faith, allowed them to preach openly. . . . When he [Ethelbert] . . . was baptized, the king encouraged [others to convert] in so far that he compelled none to embrace Christianity, but only showed more affection to the believers.

Jesus's power was emphasized, and his statement that he came to bring not peace but a sword was convenient."[13]

The church also accepted some parts of the old German religion in order to encourage acceptance of Christianity. For example, it adopted certain non-Christian customs, such as having a tree and mistletoe at Christmas. However, the church never allowed its basic structure or beliefs to be changed.

Monks and Monasteries

The most effective of the missionaries were monks, who were members of religious retreats, or monasteries. Monastery life was shaped by St. Benedict, who in 520 founded the monastery of Monte Cassino in southern Italy. Monte Cassino's code of conduct, known as St. Benedict's Rule, was adopted by most other Early Middle Ages monasteries in western Europe. The Rule insisted on strict discipline and complete obedience to the monastery's regulations. Those regulations required all members to give up their property, money, and even personal clothing. Monks were to spend their time in religious worship and in work that made the monastery as self-sufficient as possible.

In short, the monastery was to be a refuge from the world at large. It was to be a place where its members could practice, without distractions, the purest Christian life.

Monks and the Outside World

However, that isolation proved impossible to maintain. As the scholar R. Allen Brown notes, "Institutions such as these . . . attracted the most ardent and many of the most intelligent spirits of the age. But the world could not spare them nor could they be deaf to the world's needs."[14] These "intelligent spirits" might wish to isolate themselves from society, but society needed their skills and services too much for such isolation to be allowed. For instance, monks provided both health care and welfare, managing the only hospitals and orphanages in much of Europe during this time. Even the church itself had need of the talents of the monks, who as part of the clergy found themselves called on to be bishops and, in the case of Gregory I, pope.

Monks also played important roles in civil government, for they were among the small number of western Europeans who could read and write during the Early Middle Ages. Thus, they wrote letters and kept records and became the advisers of kings and other medieval rulers.

Monastery Schools

Although all these activities were important to the developing society of the Early Middle Ages, the monastery and the monk had a much more profound effect in the culture. According to historian C. Warren Hollister: "Above all, as islands of learning and security in an ocean of ignorance and political chaos,

the . . . monasteries were the spiritual and intellectual centers of the developing . . . European civilization. In short, . . . monasticism became the supreme civilizing influence in the early Christian west."[15]

Much of this civilizing influence was the product of schools run by monasteries whose monks were the teachers. For instance, some 90 percent of those who could read and write in the five centuries

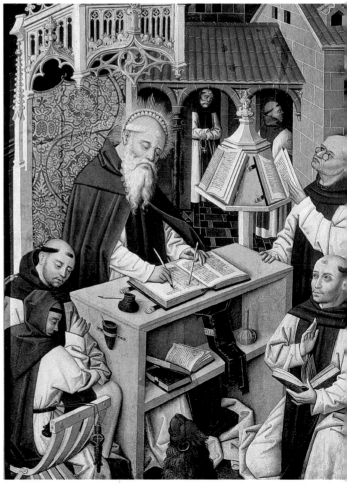

Medieval monks, shown here copying texts in a monastery, were among the few members of western European society who could read and write.

A Monk's Life

St. Benedict's Rule became the blueprint for western medieval monastic orders. Here, as quoted in *A Source Book of Medieval History*, edited by Frederic Austin Ogg, St. Benedict described some of the requirements of the monk's life.

Whether the monks should have anything of their own. More than anything else is this special vice to be cut off root and branch from the monastery. . . . [The monk] should have absolutely not anything, neither a book, nor tablets [on which to write], nor a pen—nothing at all. For indeed it is not allowed to the monks to have their own bodies or wills in their own power. But all things necessary they must expect from . . . the monastery. . . . All things shall be held in common. . . .

Concerning the daily manual labor. Idleness is the enemy of the soul. And therefore . . . the brothers [monks] ought to be occupied in manual labor; and . . . sacred reading. . . . If the . . . poverty of the place demands that they be occupied in picking fruits, they shall not be grieved; for they are truly monks if they live by the labors of their hands. . . .

Concerning the reception of guests. All guests . . . shall be received as though they were Christ . . . but most of all—to servants of the faith and to pilgrims. . . .

Whether a monk should be allowed to receive letters or anything. By no means shall it be allowed a monk—either from his relatives, or from any man, or from one of his fellows—to receive or to give, without order of the abbot, letters, presents, or any gift, however small.

following the fall of Rome were taught in monastic schools.

Additionally, these schools provided most of the religious instruction available to people of the Early Middle Ages. Even those who were able to attend church service received little from it unless they spoke Latin, the language of the church, and few in western Europe knew Latin after the fifth century.

Monastic education went beyond the central belief in salvation and promoted values that became an essential part of medieval civilization. The monks taught that self-discipline, moderation, and self-denial were virtues, as were social responsibility and charity. They saw the world as a testing ground of Christian faith and believed that the world could be made better. They further believed that God and his world could be approached through thought and study.

The Classical Heritage

These Christian principles dated back to the Roman Empire, and as Hollister notes, the monastery was "a cultural lifeline to Classical Christian antiquity."[16] The monasteries also preserved other parts of the classical past. However, their record was mixed.

Although many monasteries did preserve Roman and Greek books, they rarely saw such preservation as part of their mission, which was to create a Christian world. Additionally, although Roman books were useful in teaching Latin, many monks were horrified at constant references to Roman gods and goddesses, as well as the explicit sexual content of much Roman poetry and drama. Further, as historians David Knowles and Dimitri Obolensky point out, "it was perhaps natural to feel hostility towards a literature which was the principal attraction of a way of life that could still pose as a rival to Christianity."[17]

This hostility led to several courses of actions. Some monks were content just to remove offensive passages. Others, however, destroyed whole works they found hateful. Many monks went even further. They did not want to have anything to do with Roman and Greek writing, preferring instead original Latin works that had nothing but Christian thought in them.

This sixteenth-century illustration depicts St. Benedict receiving wheat to feed monks seated for a meal.

Many medieval monasteries maintained schools. This illustration shows students in a classroom at one such school.

On the other hand, some monks almost worshipped ancient Roman and Greek works. They saw to it that classic books were copied and recopied in monasteries throughout the Early Middle Ages, so that they survived for later scholars to use. And even the strictest Christians admired the work of the Roman poet Virgil, author of the epic poem *The Aeneid*, because of a passage in his *Eclogues* that Christians believed referred to the birth of Christ. As a result, Virgil's work survived mostly intact in western Europe and continued to be read, whereas the works of many other ancient writers disappeared completely from the region.

No matter whether sympathetic or hostile to the classical past, monks were the guardians of education and culture during the Early Middle Ages. Occasionally, others joined their effort, as happened in one German kingdom, that of the Franks in Gaul, where interest in classical works and learning created a rebirth of education and art.

Chapter Three

The Franks

At the same time that Theodoric the Great and his Ostrogoths were setting up their Italian kingdom, another Germanic tribe, the Franks, were conquering the Roman province of Gaul. Under the leadership of such kings as Clovis and Charlemagne, the Frankish state expanded. Eventually the Franks created a short-lived empire with a short-lived reawakening of art and learning.

Clovis

The Franks began their expansion from their home along the Rhine River, in what is now Holland and Belgium. In 481 Clovis, the fifteen-year-old son of a Frankish chieftain, inherited the leadership of one group of Franks. Over the next twenty-five years he united the Franks and defeated the last Roman army in Gaul. His victories left the Franks in control of Gaul and rulers of much of western Europe.

Clovis held these conquests together in two ways. First, he depended on military might to suppress dissent and rebellion. Second, he converted to Christianity, and this act made him more acceptable to the largely Christian population of Gaul. Additionally, his conversion gained him the support of the church, which in 509 officially recognized him as king of all the territory he had conquered. He thus became the first of the Merovingian dynasty, which was named after Merovech, Clovis's grandfather.

Merovingian Feuds

The Frankish kingdom did not survive Clovis's death intact, as his four sons divided up the state among themselves. This division set the stage for two centuries of struggle among the Merovingians to reunite the Franks under a single ruler. Such struggles led the Merovingians to plot against each other, stooping to every form of treachery including assassination. Gregory of Tours, a sixth-century historian, describes how Fredegund, wife of Clovis's grandson, used murder and torture in an attempt to make herself queen. After having her stepson killed, Fredegund turned on her own daughter, Rigunth, a rival for the throne.

> One day her mother . . . [said,] "Here are possessions of thy father; . . . take them. . . ." She [Fredegund] then went into her treasure-room, and opened a chest full of . . . precious ornaments. . . . Rigunth put her arm into the chest . . . when her mother seized the lid and forced it down upon her neck. She bore upon it with all her strength. . . . The attendants outside . . . broke into the . . . chamber and brought out the girl, whom they thus delivered from . . . death.[18]

Clovis, shown here being baptized, led Frankish armies to conquer much of western Europe.

This sixteenth-century painting shows Pepin the Short ceding conquered territory to the church. The alliance between Pepin and Pope Stephen II cemented Pepin's authority over the Franks.

Consumed by this constant feuding, the Merovingians had little time for ruling their domains and gradually lost power to palace officials who were the actual administrators. In the early eighth century, one of these officials, Charles Martel, became king in all but name, as he reconquered all the lands of Clovis's original kingdom. Charles was the first of the Carolingians,

a name that comes from *Carolus*, Latin for "Charles."

A Profitable Alliance

Although Charles Martel did not call himself king of the Franks, in 741 his son Pepin the Short did. Because Pepin had seized the throne from the Merovingians, he was anxious to find some way to make his rule

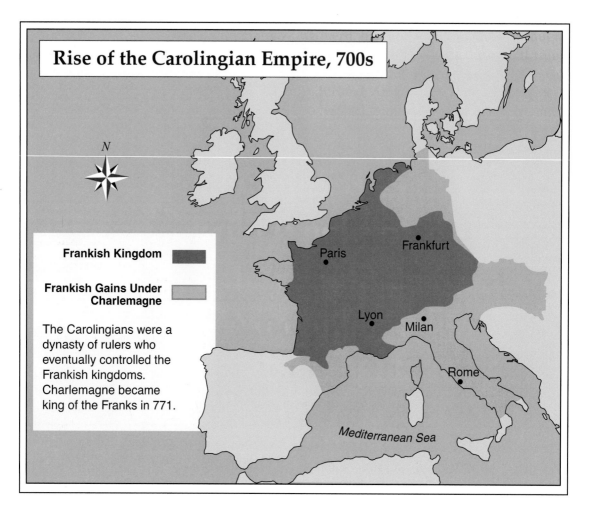

Rise of the Carolingian Empire, 700s

Frankish Kingdom

Frankish Gains Under Charlemagne

The Carolingians were a dynasty of rulers who eventually controlled the Frankish kingdoms. Charlemagne became king of the Franks in 771.

Paris

Frankfurt

Lyon

Milan

Rome

Mediterranean Sea

legitimate. In 753 Pope Stephen II offered to give the church's blessing to Pepin's rule. In exchange, the Frankish king agreed to fight the Lombards, who, notwithstanding their conversion to the Church of Rome, were extending their conquests southward toward Rome. The pope's support, as well as the ceremony at which Pepin was anointed with oil by Stephen himself, so impressed the Franks that any questions about the Carolingian's right to the throne were silenced.

After this ceremony Pepin marched to Italy, where he defeated the Lombards and gave part of their kingdom to the papacy. This land gift, known as the Donation of Pepin, was combined with the territory surrounding Rome to form the Papal States. So as well as being the spiritual leader of the western church, the pope was now the secular leader of much of central Italy. The papacy consequently profited from the income produced by the rich farmland of the region.

The papacy also profited from its alliance with the Frankish kingdom. This alliance ensured the popes' independence, for the Franks' powerful military saw to it that no one, Lombard king or Byzantine emperor, would conquer and impose rule over the pope. Nor was it likely that the Franks themselves would take over Rome. They were too busy with their growing kingdom, by this time the largest governed region in the west since the fall of the Roman Empire.

Charlemagne

The cordial relations between the Franks and the pope continued during the reign of Pepin's successor, his son Charlemagne, who ruled from 771 to 814. Charlemagne reaffirmed his father's land gift to the papacy and undertook to complete the conquest of the Lombards begun by his father.

After the Lombards, the Frankish king then turned his attention east, and in 785, after almost a decade of truly bloody war, he defeated the Saxons, another German tribe, and added their territory to his kingdom. With this addition, Charlemagne's domain was immense. It included all of modern-day France, Switzerland, the Low Countries, and much of Germany and Austria, as well as running deep into northern Italy. For many in western Europe, it seemed to be a rebirth of the old empire, even though the Frankish state did not cover quite the same lands. For the Franks, then, it was appropriate that on Christmas day in the year 800, Pope Leo III crowned Charlemagne emperor of the western Roman Empire, despite the Byzantine emperors' continuing claim to be the only Roman emperors.

The Rebirth of Education

In creating an empire, Charlemagne showed that he was an able military leader.

However, his ambitions did not end with conquest. He wanted to transform his society into something closer to that of ancient Rome. In order to do that, he had to encourage learning among his subjects—or at least the Frankish nobles.

During the first centuries of the Early Middle Ages, such skills as reading, writing, and calculating mostly disappeared in western Europe. Teachers and schools were luxuries that people struggling to survive could not afford. Additionally, education generally was not valued in the young German kingdoms, whose leaders could see little practical use in being able to write or figure.

Charlemagne, on the other hand, saw education in a different light. He realized that the survival of his domain depended upon such skills as writing and calculating because someone had to keep records and accounts. Without written records there was no way to know even the most basic things, such as how much money the state had. So Charlemagne set up schools throughout his domain. One of these schools was at the palace, and Charlemagne himself attended it to learn how to read. Unfortunately, he never mastered writing.

Charlemagne's enthusiasm for education was inherited by his successors. His son, Louis the Pious, had a palace school, and the court of Charlemagne's grandson Charles the Bald was famous for its religious discussions and debates.

Alcuin

The actual work of setting up the Carolingian schools was done by the English monk Alcuin. Before his recruitment by

Portrait of an Emperor

In his Life of Charles the Great, *excerpted in* A Source Book of Medieval History, *edited by Frederic Austin Ogg, Charlemagne's secretary Einhard provides the following portrait of the Frankish ruler:*

Charles was large and strong . . . though not . . . tall. . . . His eyes [were] very large and animated . . . hair auburn. . . . His appearance was always . . . dignified, . . . although his . . . [stomach was] prominent. . . . He took frequent exercise on horseback . . . and often indulged in swimming. . . .

He sometimes carried a jeweled sword, but only on great feast-days. . . . On great feast-days he made use of embroidered clothes; . . . but on other days his dress differed little from ordinary people. . . .

Charles had the gift of ready and fluent speech, and could express whatever he had to say with the utmost clearness. [He gave] attention to the study of foreign languages. . . . He took lessons in grammar. . . . The king spent much time and labor . . . studying. . . . He learned to make calculations. . . . He also tried to write, and used to keep tablets [for writing] . . . in bed under his pillow. . . .

He cherished . . . the principles of the Christian religion. . . . He was a constant worshipper . . . going morning and evening. . . . He was very active in aiding the poor . . . he not only . . . [gave] in . . . his kingdom, but . . . [also to] Christians living in poverty in Syria, Egypt, and Africa. . . . The wish that he had nearest his heart was to re-establish the ancient authority of the city of Rome . . . and to defend and protect the Church.

Charlemagne, the son of Pepin, became sole ruler of the Franks in 771 and was crowned emperor of the western Roman Empire in 800.

Charlemagne, Alcuin had been the head of the most advanced school in western Europe, a sort of early university. Because of his reputation, he was able to lure teachers from Italy, Britain, and Spain. Further, one of Alcuin's students, Raban Maur, became a classical scholar who made the monastery school at Fulda in present-day Germany the best in western Europe.

One of the English monk's greatest achievements was to make the reading of handwritten documents easier. Before Alcuin, handwriting was very difficult to make out because letters were poorly formed and words were generally run together. Alcuin introduced a system that eliminated these problems by using small, clearly made, uniform letters and by inserting spaces between words.

Thus, Alcuin was the most important figure in the Carolingian rebirth of education. As historian Norman F. Cantor notes, "he established . . . schools . . . [and] libraries. . . . He wrote textbooks . . . [and] prepared word lists. The impact of his work can be seen in the great increase of literary and documentary materials surviving from the Carolingian period."[19]

Reviving Art

This reawakening of learning was part of the Carolingian renaissance, which also saw a renewed interest in the arts. During the sixth, seventh, and eighth centuries, there had been a dramatic decrease in the production of art, music, and literature in western Europe. This decline was due to the economic collapse that followed the fall of the western Roman Empire. Fewer ways of making money, particularly through trade, meant fewer wealthy people, whom artists, musicians, and writers had depended upon in the ancient world to support their work. In the first centuries of the Early Middle Ages, what passed for wealthy aristocrats in the German kingdoms had no time for art. Their sole objective in life was to wage war. In the Frankish state, however, Charlemagne changed that attitude by sponsoring writers and artists.

In keeping with Charlemagne's desire to revive the Roman Empire, Carolingian artists looked to the ancient empire for inspiration. As a result, painters showed their people in Roman clothes, a practice that remained popular throughout the Middle Ages. Roman-inspired architects reintroduced the standard Roman public building, the cross-shaped basilica. They did, however, add some original features, most notably a front that either featured two towers or had a fortresslike appearance. The exact significance of this addition is unknown, but these front sections contained a complex of rooms under whose floors important people were buried.

Carolingian authors likewise were influenced by ancient Rome. They wrote not in their native German but in Latin, the language of the old empire. The poets modeled their work closely on the verse forms popular among the Romans, particularly favoring short lyric poems on such subjects as gardening, winter, and baldness (in honor of Charles the Bald). Prose was exclusively nonfiction—histories and biographies that imitated in form those of Plutarch and other

ancient writers and took as their subjects the Franks and their leaders, especially Charlemagne. The accuracy of these works remains suspect as they were meant to be propaganda that promoted the idea that the Franks were the natural successors of the Romans and that Charlemagne and his heirs were God's appointed rulers.

Other Flowerings

The Carolingian renaissance was not the only gush of art and learning in western Europe, although it was the most far-reaching. Like Charlemagne, other leaders in the young German kingdoms looked back with longing at the accomplishments of the Romans and wished to revive that ancient culture's art and learning.

The English monk Alcuin (pictured to the right of Charlemagne, on throne) set up schools and introduced an improved system of handwriting, leading to a rebirth of education during Charlemagne's reign.

In seventh-century Spain, the Visigoths set up schools that taught the ancient classics, which they imitated in their own writing. In keeping with this fascination with the past, Isidore, bishop of Seville, went beyond imitation and lifted whole passages out of the works of Roman authors in his writings on language and religion.

Following in the footsteps of the Visigoths and the Carolingians, Alfred the Great, king of southern England in the ninth century, financed schools. The scholar Will Durant observes that "an eighth of his [Alfred's] revenue was devoted to education. At Reading, his capital, he established a palace school, and gave abundantly to the educational . . . work of churches and monasteries. . . . He sent abroad for scholars . . . to come and instruct his people and himself."[20]

Short-Lived Endeavors

In the end, the efforts by the Carolingians and other western Europeans to revive education and art on a large scale failed. Most people had no room in their lives for education or art; for them, just growing enough to eat was a full-time job. Additionally, war and invasion were too common to provide the necessary stability to support artists, writers, and teachers.

Still, the very effort by the German kingdoms to revive art and learning established their importance in the minds of many people. Eventually, the recognition of the need for both would give rise to a permanent renaissance of art and education in the Late Middle Ages.

Imperial Collapse

Just as Charlemagne's renaissance failed to revive art and learning, so his empire failed to restore Rome. Indeed, the Frankish

Charlemagne on Education

In the following letter, written sometime before 800 and quoted in A Source Book of Medieval History, *edited by Frederic Austin Ogg, Charlemagne reveals to the Abbot Baugulf of the monastery of Fulda his belief that education must play a major role in religion.*

Monasteries . . . should be zealous . . . in the cherishing of letters [reading and writing] and in teaching those who . . . are able to learn. . . . So that . . . those who wish to please God by living rightly should not fail to please Him also by speaking correctly. For it is written, "Either from thy words thou shall be justified or from thy words thou shalt be condemned." . . . In recent years when letters have been written to us from monasteries, . . . we have recognized . . . both correct thoughts and uncouth expressions. . . . We began to fear that, . . . as the skill of writing was less, so also the wisdom for understanding the Holy Scriptures might be much less than it rightly ought to be.

empire ended only a quarter century after Charlemagne's death in 814. Its breakup was unavoidable because in western Europe there was no way of organizing or running such a large state in the Early Middle Ages. The political and economic institutions no longer existed. Further, the Carolingian empire simply did not have enough talented and committed leaders to survive intact. Cantor writes that "the death of only a few enlightened leaders, or even the sudden loss of one great personality, can cause the whole system to collapse and open the way for . . . [a rapid] reversion to chaos and barbarism."[21]

An additional factor leading to the breakup of Charlemagne's state was rivalry among the Carolingian heirs. Charlemagne had only one surviving son, Louis

the Pious, so the empire passed intact to him. However, when Louis died in 840, he had three sons. His desire was for his oldest son, Lothair, to become emperor and to rule the entire Frankish state. According to Louis's will, Lothair's two brothers, Charles the Bald and Louis the German, were to assist the new emperor as kings in the west and east.

It pleased us [Louis the Pious] . . . to crown him [Lothair] . . . with the imperial diadem [crown], and to appoint him our . . . successor to the Empire. . . . It was . . . agreed to confer upon his brothers . . . the title of King, and to determine the places . . . in which . . . they shall wield power under their elder brother. . . . We wish the two brothers who bear the title of

King to have power of their own to distribute all honors within their dominion.[22]

The younger brothers, however, did not want to serve under Lothair. They, therefore, formed an alliance and attacked the emperor. In 843, after a year-long war, Charles and Louis forced Lothair to sign the Treaty of Verdun, which divided the Frankish empire into three parts.

The result of the Treaty of Verdun was the loss of whatever unity the Frankish empire had gained from its short existence. Under the treaty's terms Charles received a large region that became France within a few centuries and Louis a similarly sized territory that became Germany. Lothair, the emperor, was left with a thin strip of territory that ran north and south between the much larger kingdoms of his two brothers. This imperial strip was caught in a tug-of-war between the other two kingdoms, and even after the strip ceased to be a single state, it remained a prize over which France and Germany would fight for centuries during the Middle Ages.

This church in modern-day Germany features the two towers that were typical of the Roman-inspired architecture during the reign of Charlemagne.

This illustration shows Charlemagne's death in 814. Squabbles among his descendants led to the breakup of his once-vast empire nearly three decades later.

Emperor Against Emperor

In 871 Emperor Louis II, Charlemagne's great-grandson, wrote to Byzantine emperor Basil I. Louis's letter, reprinted in Sources for the History of Medieval Europe, *edited by Brian Pullan, defends his right to call himself a Roman emperor.*

It is ridiculous of you [Basil I] to say that the [western] imperial title is . . . [not] hereditary. . . . In what way is it not hereditary?—for our grandfather was already inheriting it from his father. . . .

   You profess to be astonished that we call ourselves Emperors, not of the Franks, but of the Romans: but . . . we could not be Emperors of the Franks without being Emperors of the Romans. We took over this title . . . from the Romans; . . . and we received from heaven this people and this city [Rome] to guide and the mother of all churches of God to defend. . . . From her [the western church] the founder of our line received the authority. . . . Men have frequently risen to be Emperor . . . not by any divine operation carried out by the pontiff; but only from the Senate and the people. . . . Some have not even risen by this means, for they have been . . . set upon the imperial throne by the soldiers, and some of them have even been promoted by . . . other dubious means.

The Legacy of Charlemagne

Despite the collapse of his empire, Charlemagne left a legacy that proved crucial to the Early Middle Ages. The scholar David Nicholas writes that "although the unification of Europe . . . was a personal achievement that survived only a generation after his death, Charlemagne's transformation of local institutions was to survive . . . throughout the Middle Ages."[23]

   The most important of these transformations was the Frankish emperor's strengthening and refining of the feudal system. This act was his most important contribution to medieval culture because it was feudalism that bound western European society together for the rest of the Middle Ages.

Chapter Four

Feudalism

Feudalism was the economic and political system under which western Europe operated through much of the Middle Ages. It began to take shape in the first centuries of the Early Middle Ages under the first Frankish kings, and by the time of Charlemagne the system existed in broad outline, with one noble pledging to serve another, particularly in war, in exchange for certain rights, such as the use of large farming estates. Historian Crane Brinton notes that its growth was in response to "the breakdown of . . . rulers' ability to hold together large groups of human beings for political or economic purposes. The One World of Roman law, administration, and business was shattered into hundreds, indeed thousands, of little local units."[24]

Social Order

Before the fall of the western Roman empire, the imperial bureaucracy had given order to society by passing along com-

mands from the emperor and senate to all the regions of the empire. Imperial administrators scattered across the empire saw that these commands were obeyed. In this way the central government maintained order through supervision and control.

However, the society of the Franks, like German society in general, was based on the tribe and, therefore, it had no political institutions designed to organize and govern a large state. For the Franks, feudalism provided the necessary social order that had disappeared with the western empire. It also created a new chain of command to replace the one that was gone.

Lords and Vassals

The chain that bound feudal society together was a mutually beneficial bargain

This sixth-century Spanish illustration shows a vassal bowing to his lord. The feudal system helped bring order to European society after the collapse of the Roman Empire.

entered into by two aristocrats. One noble, known as the vassal (Celtic for "servant"), pledged to carry out a number of duties, of which the most important was military service. In exchange for these services, the other, called the lord, or suzerain (Latin for "the one above"), then provided the vassal with protection, as well as a way of taking care of such basic needs as food and clothing.

Nothing kept lords from being vassals to other nobles nor kept vassals from being lords. In fact, points out the scholar François L. Ganshof, most nobles were both: "It is . . . very important to realize that vassals . . . would normally acquire other vassals for their own service. This would often . . . be done at their [own] lord's . . . desire, since in this way, they could raise a large number of fighting men for his service."[25]

The Oath of Fealty

The pledge that the vassal gave was the oath of fealty, or fidelity. It was a straightforward agreement:

> To that magnificent lord. . . . Your good will has decreed . . . that I should hand myself over . . . to your guardianship, . . . that you should aid me . . . as well as with food as with clothing. . . . And so long as I shall live I ought to provide service and honor to you, . . . and I shall not during the time of my life have the ability to withdraw from your power or guardianship.[26]

The bond created by this pledge between suzerain and vassal could be broken by a lord who found a vassal guilty of not meeting his obligations. The lord then stripped the vassal of all rights and of the lord's protection. It was harder for a vassal to break the feudal contract. Indeed, it was illegal for a vassal to leave his lord except for such major violations of fealty as the lord's trying to kill him.

Duties and Responsibilities

The receiving and giving of the oath of fealty imposed specific duties and rights on both lord and vassal. A lord promised to protect his vassal and the vassal's property. Such duties might require the lord to raise an army if a vassal were faced with an enemy too large for his own forces to handle. The lord also pledged to see that a vassal accused of breaking his oath—or any other crime—would have the chance to plead his case before his social equals, or peers.

In return, the vassal swore to give advice on political and military matters both to the lord and to other vassals of the lord. The vassal also promised to provide his lord with aid, particularly military aid. Thus, if his lord commanded, the vassal, fully equipped with armor and weapons, had to go to war. In many instances, he also had to provide soldiers for his lord's army. However, to keep warfare from being too time-consuming and costly, this military service was normally limited to forty days a year.

The vassal's oath might further require him to lodge and feed his lord, along with the lord's household. Again, to keep this form of aid from becoming too heavy a burden, the lord's stay was limited.

The final form of aid that a vassal might have to provide was money when the lord needed it. Emergencies, long wars, or important events, such as the marriage of the lord's oldest daughter or the knighting of his eldest son, called for such financial aid.

Honorable Service

Both lords and vassals, as well as members of their households, believed that nothing was more important than being a good vassal and fulfilling feudal obligations. In the following letter, written in 843,

A nobleman swears fealty to a lord in this panel of the Bayeux Tapestry, an eleventh-century work that portrays key events in medieval history.

a Frankish mother explains to her son how he can best serve his lord:

I exhort you to maintain faithfully all that is in your charge, with all your strength of body and soul, as long as your life shall last. . . . Show yourself towards your lord . . . [as] true, vigilant, useful, and prompt to his service. In every matter which concerns the power and welfare of [your lord] . . . show that wisdom that God has plentifully endowed you.[27]

To the Frankish nobility, vassalage was an honor and not one lightly given. Indeed, only members of the upper class were allowed to become vassals. Thus, nobles took the oath of fealty, as did high-ranking church officials—bishops and abbots. No one else, including the lower clergy, could be a vassal, and even among the upper class, not everyone was a vassal, although most were.

Women and Feudalism

There was one group among the aristocracy whose members were prohibited

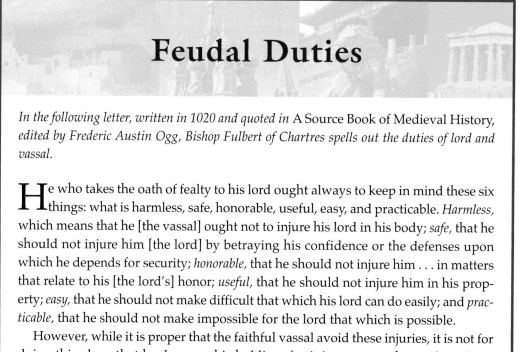

Feudal Duties

In the following letter, written in 1020 and quoted in A Source Book of Medieval History, *edited by Frederic Austin Ogg, Bishop Fulbert of Chartres spells out the duties of lord and vassal.*

He who takes the oath of fealty to his lord ought always to keep in mind these six things: what is harmless, safe, honorable, useful, easy, and practicable. *Harmless,* which means that he [the vassal] ought not to injure his lord in his body; *safe,* that he should not injure him [the lord] by betraying his confidence or the defenses upon which he depends for security; *honorable,* that he should not injure him . . . in matters that relate to his [the lord's] honor; *useful,* that he should not injure him in his property; *easy,* that he should not make difficult that which his lord can do easily; and *practicable,* that he should not make impossible for the lord that which is possible.

However, while it is proper that the faithful vassal avoid these injuries, it is not for doing this alone that he deserves his holding; for it is not enough to refrain from wrongdoing, unless that which is good is done also. . . . Therefore, . . . in the same six things referred to above he should faithfully advise and aid his lord. . . .

The lord also ought to act toward his faithful vassal in the same manner in all these things. And if he fails to do this, he will be rightfully regarded as guilty of bad faith, just as the former [would be], if he should be found shirking . . . his obligations.

from being vassals: women. Nor could women accept an oath of fealty. However, aristocratic women did have some rights under the feudal system. As historian David Nicholas writes, upperclass women of the Early Middle Ages could "inherit on the same basis as men. . . . The open society of early Frankish Gaul permitted some women to rise to positions of influence."[28]

Still, a woman's rights were generally tied to her being a wife or daughter. For instance, a woman could inherit her father's property only if she were married. The only place where women were really in charge and could direct their own affairs was in a nunnery, the female counterpart of a monastery.

The Authority of Kings

The feudal system from which women were excluded had a hierarchy shaped like a pyramid with the king at the top. On the level below the king were his personal vassals, who were themselves lords to others below them. The pyramid continued on down to vassals who had no vassals of their own.

The feudal pyramid suggests that the higher up a noble was in the hierarchy, the more powerful he was, with the king being the most powerful of all. The reality, however, was that vassals were often more powerful than their lords because the vassals generally had more direct control over soldiers than did the lords.

During Merovingian times, the king lacked direct authority over most of the aristocrats of his realm. For instance, if he wished to raise an army for war, he

A fourteenth-century illustration shows an upper-class husband and wife. Women had little social or political status in the feudal system.

ordered his vassals to arm themselves. The royal vassals in turn ordered their vassals to war and so on down the feudal pyramid. If any noble below the king's own vassals balked and refused to serve, the king had no way of forcing the disobedient one to obey. Another problem for the

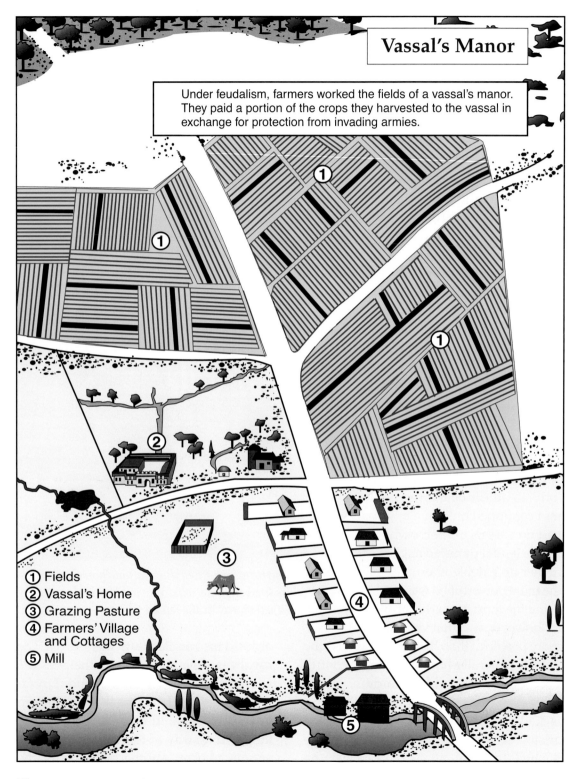

Vassal's Manor

Under feudalism, farmers worked the fields of a vassal's manor. They paid a portion of the crops they harvested to the vassal in exchange for protection from invading armies.

① Fields
② Vassal's Home
③ Grazing Pasture
④ Farmers' Village and Cottages
⑤ Mill

Merovingian ruler was that many of the most powerful Frankish aristocrats were not his vassals or vassals of anyone else. They sat atop their own hierarchies that paralleled the king's.

Increased Power

When Charlemagne became ruler of the Franks, he desired to increase his direct authority over and strengthen his hold on the nobility. Consequently, he sought to have every noble's first oath of fealty be to him. In exchange for this fealty, the emperor gave each vassal a benefice (Latin for "benefit"), later called a fief (meaning "fee"), from which the term *feudal* comes. A benefice or fief was a grant that supplied the vassal with income.

By granting fiefs, Charlemagne and his successors were able to make vassals out of even the nobles who had previously been free of vassalage. As Ganshof observes, "The . . . Carolingians, by distributing . . . the wealth . . . attracted members of higher social levels into the ranks of their vassals. A steadily growing proportion of members of the aristocracy, including . . . the counts, were now prepared to become vassals of the king."[29] As an additional inducement for pledging fealty to them, the Carolingians eventually allowed fiefs to be inherited. The vassal's heir had to pay a form of inheritance tax called relief to his lord. This relief could be as much money as the fief produced in a year. For vassals who died without heirs, the fief was the lord's to dispose of as he saw fit.

The Fief

There were many different kinds of fiefs, for a fief could be anything that generated revenue for the vassal: a mill for grinding grain, a house that could be rented, or a toll bridge. Although most fiefs were based on property, in a few cases a vassal's fief might have nothing to do with property but rather allow him to gather taxes or assign and collect fines. And some vassals, who lived with their lord and were known as household retainers, received actual money as their fief.

The most common type of fief was a tract of land that contained one or more farming estates, known as manors. Such land grants could vary in size from a few hundred to tens of thousands of acres. The former, a single manor, went to ordinary knights, while the latter went to high-ranking vassals, such as counts and barons. A vassal who controlled more than one manor could, and often did, attract vassals of his own by offering them one of these manors as a fief.

The Manor Community

The layout of the manor was fairly standard, with each estate spreading out from the vassal's home, which was a large house or a castle. Workers' cottages clustered nearby, as did the occasional village, all being surrounded by pastures, croplands, and woodlands.

Many manors used what was called the three-field system for raising crops. Each year, one field was used for spring planting, one for fall, and one was left unused. Use of the fields would rotate from year to year so that each field had time to rest and recover from being worked. The fields were divided into long strips, each separated from its neighbors by unplowed land. Fences were never used.

Each manor supplied most of the needs of the people living on it. However, like any farming community, a manor sometimes had too much of some foods and not enough of others. Also, estates often specialized. Thus, some grew grain crops, while others raised sheep, pigs, and cattle. To balance out the excesses and shortages, as well as from specialization, trade between manors arose.

The Lord of the Manor

The fief-holder, known as the landlord, lived with his household, which consist-ed of his family and retainers. How much income the manor produced determined the size of the landlord's household, which in turn set the number of soldiers that he had to provide his suzerain.

Caring for the household were servants such as cooks, waiters, grooms, and huntsmen. Also, each manor had a priest, with very rich manors having several, one of whom was assigned solely to the landlord's household.

Manor Income

The lord of the manor made money from his estate in a variety of ways. Above all else, he enjoyed the income from rents

On the Early Death of a Vassal

The following instructions, reprinted in A Source Book of Medieval History, *edited by Frederic Austin Ogg, detail the arrangements necessary for the protection of a dead vassal's underage children.*

Heirs should be placed in guardianship until they reach the age of twenty years. . . .

When a female ward reaches the proper age to marry, she should be married by the advice and consent of her lord, and by the advice and consent of her relatives and friends, according as the nobility of her ancestry and the value of her fief may require; and upon her marriage the fief which has been held in guardianship should be given over to her. A woman cannot be freed from wardship except by marriage. . . .

The fiefs of those who are under wardship should be cared for attentively by their lords, who are entitled to receive the produce and profits. And in this connection let it be known that the lord ought to preserve in their former condition the buildings, the manor-houses, the forests, and meadows, . . . the mills, the fisheries, and the other things of which he has the profits. And he should not sell, destroy, or remove the woods, houses, or the trees.

paid by farmworkers living on the land. These rents generally came in the form of crops, livestock, and cut timber. In addition, any surplus production on the estate also belonged to the landlord. He either sold the food and materials or kept them for his own use.

The vassal also charged his tenants to keep sheep or pigs. He made more money from fees paid by farmworkers to grind their corn at the manor's mill and bake their bread at the manor's ovens. The landlord collected other fees from tenants sending their children to school or to an apprentice to learn a trade.

Some vassals had a final source of revenue from their estates when along with a manor a king awarded a vassal immunity. Immunity meant that no royal official could collect taxes or try criminals on that property. Rather, the vassal collected his own taxes, which he spent as he wished. Further, he made his own laws, running his own courts and levying fines. According to the scholar Rowland E. Prothero, the number of "fees and fines levied by the manorial courts in the course of a year was surprisingly large. . . . Here . . . were imposed the fines for slovenly work, . . . for selling cattle without the lord's leave [permission], . . . for neglecting to repair a cottage. . . . Here the miller would be fined for mixing rubbish with his flour."[30]

This woodcut shows a medieval tenant paying rent to his landlord. Such rents often were paid in goods and services rather than currency.

Serfs and Other Peasants

Most of the inhabitants of the manor were peasants, the majority of whom were serfs (Latin for "slave"). Serfs were mostly farmhands, although some did other jobs, such as blacksmithing. A serf paid the lord of the manor for the right to live and work on the manor. Serfs were not vassals because, being peasants and thus members of a lower social class, they could not offer an oath of fealty to the aristocratic lord of the manor.

A serf had little freedom. Without his landlord's permission a serf could not leave the manor, could not change his job, and could not marry someone from another manor. Yet despite these restrictions, serfs were not slaves. They could not be bought and sold, and a serf's position was as hereditary as that of any noble. As part of this inheritance, serfs remained on the same manor and farmed the same land as had their ancestors. Further, unlike slaves, serfs had rights. For example, they could not be stripped of their land as long as they performed all their required work.

In addition to the serfs, some of the manor's inhabitants were freemen, peasants who owned the land they worked and owed little to the landlord. Additionally, there were always some landless workers among the manor's peasants.

Profitable Enterprises

The labor of serfs and free peasants made most manors productive and therefore very profitable for their landlords. This profitability naturally made estates the most sought-after of fiefs. Indeed, manors were

so valuable that nobles who had not already been awarded the use of several manors won control of multiple estates by giving oaths of fealty to more than one lord. These multiple oaths, however, led to much confusion as to which lord should be served first. A vassal with two lords, for instance, might be called upon for military service by both at the same time. Initially, there was no rule to help the vassal decide which lord's demand took prece-

Peasants work on a manor in this sixteenth-century illustration.

Feudal Immunity

Under feudalism vassals often received immunity, which allowed them to be free of outside interference in running their fiefs. In the following excerpt, found in Sources for the History of Medieval Europe, *edited by Brian Pullan, the Frankish ruler Louis the Pious grants immunity to the Abbot Arnulf.*

All our loyal servants, both present and future, shall know . . . that we have deemed the petition of . . . Abbot Arnulf worthy to be heard by us . . . and have taken the . . . monastery under our protection and that of immunity. . . .

We therefore command . . . that no public judge . . . shall dare . . . to enter the churches, places, fields, or other possessions which the said monastery . . . hold . . . for the purpose of hearing and discussing cases in the manner of a judge, or of exacting fines, . . . or of . . . claiming hospitality there . . . , or of taking . . . horses . . . , or of wrongfully coercing the men of the monastery who live upon its land, whether they are free-men or serfs; or in order to demand payment of taxes. . . . And . . . we entirely remit [excuse] . . . the . . . monastery any dues the public treasury could expect to be paid out of the monastery's property, so that this [the monastery's profits] increase to provide alms to the poor and to support the monks.

dence. The eventual solution was to name one lord the vassal's chief lord, or liege lord.

Not all aristocrats found it necessary to offer multiple oaths of fealty in order to increase their holdings. Some with enough soldiers simply went to war and seized the lands they desired. No traditions, laws, court cases, or legal thinking put a stop to these private wars.

Yet despite such drawbacks, feudal society provided enough stability and order that it continued among the Franks and eventually spread beyond them. By the Late Middle Ages feudalism was established in every part of western and much of eastern Europe. Nevertheless, one European power remained outside the feudal system, maintaining itself in much the manner of the old Romans. This was the Byzantine Empire.

Chapter Five

The Byzantines

While the Franks and other Germans were creating kingdoms out of the western Roman Empire, the eastern half, renamed the Byzantine Empire by modern historians, continued to exist. The eastern empire had survived because, according to scholar David Nicholas, "population density and . . . wealth were much higher in the east than in the west."[31] These advantages made it possible for the Byzantines to have a large army and bureaucracy, both necessary to protect and run the empire. An additional advantage was that the eastern empire was more compact than the western. Thus, all imperial regions could be reached swiftly in times of trouble.

Because of its wealth, political stability, and size, the Byzantine Empire was the most powerful European state during the Early Middle Ages. Further, unlike the German kingdoms, it also retained much of its ancient classical heritage and was a center for art and learning.

The Greek Empire

The capital of the Byzantine Empire was Constantinople (present-day Istanbul). Named for the Emperor Constantine I, who made it the capital of the eastern empire in the fourth century A.D., the city was also known as Byzantium, from the name of its legendary founder, Byzas. The city sat in what was then Greece on the European side of the Bosporus, the narrow northernmost section of the straits that link the Black Sea to the Mediterranean.

Because the Byzantines ruled from Greece and used Greek rather than Latin as their official language, western Europeans viewed the empire as Greek. Nonetheless, the Byzantines continued calling themselves Romans because they always thought of themselves as the heirs to the Roman Empire.

The Emperor

In keeping with this Roman heritage, an emperor sat at the top of the Byzantine government and society. The Byzantine ruler was the most powerful individual in the empire. His decrees automatically became laws, which no one in the empire could overturn.

In addition to ruling the Byzantine state, the emperor was also head of the eastern church. As a result, any crime against the church was a crime against the state. Among the emperor's religious duties was chairing church councils and nominating candidates to be the patriarch of Constantinople, the ranking bishop of the eastern church.

Governing the Empire

The emperor had help running the Byzantine state. He was briefed daily on both secular and religious matters by civil and church officials. All government departments operated under his direct order because only the emperor had the authority to set policy. It was the emperor who, among other things, determined the

The emperor Constantine I (left) made Constantinople, also known as Byzantium, the capital of the eastern Roman empire in the fourth century A.D.

The Third Council of Constantinople, pictured here, was called by Byzantine emperor Constantine IV in an attempt to reconcile differences between the eastern and western Christian churches.

amount of tax the average citizen paid, ordered army units from one imperial post to another, and decided how much would be spent on erecting new buildings in Constantinople.

The emperor had a number of hand-picked personal advisers who formed a cabinet. At regularly scheduled meetings, the emperor and his cabinet discussed administrative appointments, problems at home and abroad, proposed laws, and daily management of imperial affairs.

Among these personal advisers, on occasion, was the emperor's wife. Some empresses sat in on cabinet meetings or took care of day-to-day imperial duties. The sixth-century emperor Justinian I went even further and gave his wife, Theodora, the right to issue orders in his name when she proved to be a very able administrator.

In addition to his personal advisers, the emperor also had the aid of the Byzantine senate, which was modeled on that of Rome. The senate drew up legislation and presented it to the emperor, who might or might not accept it. The senate had no power to pass laws of its own.

Elections and Revolts

Emperors chose their successors since the emperorship was not hereditary. Most emperors chose a son as imperial heir, but some selected a close and trusted friend or adviser. However, the naming of an heir did not automatically make the candidate the imperial heir. In this one area the emperor was not supreme because the successor had to be approved by majority vote by three groups—the senate, the army, and the citizens of the empire. If any two of these groups voted against the candidate, the emperor had to select another successor.

These three bodies of electors could also vote to remove an incompetent or unpopular emperor; it only took the majority vote of one group. Nevertheless, most emperors who lost their thrones were overthrown by armed revolt. Revolts against the imperial ruler were common, and over the centuries, emperors were killed, imprisoned, and exiled. Many were also blinded, an act that made them unacceptable to hold the throne.

Military Might

Despite these outbreaks of civil unrest, the Byzantine Empire was always strong enough to resist attack by various nomadic tribes who came out of central Asia. Although some invaders, such as the Magyars, did conquer parts of eastern Europe, successful Byzantine resistance kept them from turning their full attention toward western Europe. Thus, the western kingdoms of the Franks and other Germans were protected from being overrun by these eastern invaders.

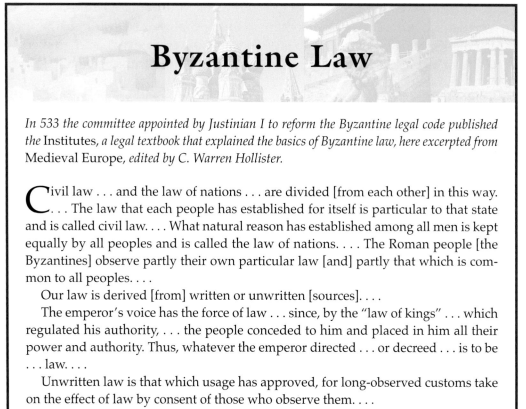

Byzantine Law

In 533 the committee appointed by Justinian I to reform the Byzantine legal code published the Institutes, *a legal textbook that explained the basics of Byzantine law, here excerpted from* Medieval Europe, *edited by C. Warren Hollister.*

Civil law . . . and the law of nations . . . are divided [from each other] in this way. . . . The law that each people has established for itself is particular to that state and is called civil law. . . . What natural reason has established among all men is kept equally by all peoples and is called the law of nations. . . . The Roman people [the Byzantines] observe partly their own particular law [and] partly that which is common to all peoples. . . .

Our law is derived [from] written or unwritten [sources]. . . .

The emperor's voice has the force of law . . . since, by the "law of kings" . . . which regulated his authority, . . . the people conceded to him and placed in him all their power and authority. Thus, whatever the emperor directed . . . or decreed . . . is to be . . . law. . . .

Unwritten law is that which usage has approved, for long-observed customs take on the effect of law by consent of those who observe them. . . .

And, natural laws, which are followed by all nations alike, deriving from divine providence, remain always firm and unchangeable; . . . those which each state constitutes for itself [are] often subject to alteration.

The Byzantines were able to defend themselves so well because they had an excellent army and navy. Careful training went along with strong, well-made steel swords, spears, and armor. The Byzantines had a signal corps that used mirrors to flash messages back and forth, an ambulance corps, and an efficient intelligence corps.

Further, the Byzantines had one of the first secret weapons, Greek fire. Although its exact nature is now unknown, Greek fire probably contained petroleum. It was pumped into bronze lion heads mounted on ships and then shot across the water to set enemy vessels afire. It was a fearsome weapon that ignited when exposed to air and could not be put out with water.

The Economy

Upkeep of the Byzantine military was expensive, but the empire could afford the expense because the realm was wealthy. The imperial economy was so strong that the *nomisma*, the Byzantine gold piece, was the standard coin throughout the entire Mediterranean region for over eight hundred years, well into the Late Middle Ages.

One of the major sources of Byzantine wealth was trade. Constantinople was perfectly positioned to control trade moving north and south from the Black Sea to the Mediterranean and east and west across the Bosporus. The most profitable trade goods that passed through the empire were silk, purple dye, and gold embroidery, all used for the ceremonial clothing

The Byzantines used a secret weapon known as Greek fire to ignite enemy vessels during sea battles.

of secular and religious leaders in both the east and the west.

Also important to the imperial treasury were successful state-owned businesses and industries, such as farms, cattle ranches, and marble quarries. The rest of the empire's income came from property and inheritance taxes.

Education

Byzantine wealth was spent on more than the imperial military. It also supported the empire's many schools. The Byzantines had inherited from their Greek and Roman ancestors a deep love and respect for learning. As a result, every Byzantine desired a good education and viewed the lack of one as a serious handicap.

Consequently, although learning was confined in the west almost exclusively to monasteries, in the east it was pursued in a large variety of secular schools, including the imperial university at Constantinople. Nicholas writes that "primary education was available even in some smaller villages for both sexes: although formal higher education was normally restricted to men, many aristocratic women studied under tutors."[32]

Most people in the upper and middle classes learned to read and write at a time when few in the west, even among the elite, could do either. They learned these skills by studying classical Greek and Latin works, most of which, unlike in the west, were preserved in the many libraries of the empire. Historian Crane Brinton observes that "had it not been for Byzantium, it seems certain that Plato and Aristotle, Homer and Sophocles would have been lost. We cannot even imagine what such a loss would have meant to western civilization."[33]

High Culture

In addition to education and the military, Byzantine riches went to the arts, with wealthy patrons plentiful among the merchants and aristocrats of the empire. The emperor also sponsored artists and writers.

One of the arts at which the Byzantines excelled was architecture. Constantinople, in particular, was filled with impressive public buildings, such as the sixth-century Church of Santa Sophia. The architects of Santa Sophia took the standard Roman public building, the cross-shaped basilica, and combined it with the dome popular in the Middle East. The result was a new type of church that the Byzantine historian Procopius said made "one feel at once that it is the work not of man's effort, . . . but . . . the work of the divine power; and the spirit . . . realizes that here God is very near."[34]

Besides architecture, the Byzantines were very skilled at painting, mosaics, gold and silver working, and ivory carving. They produced elaborate silks and jeweled book covers, and their illustrated books were the models for the important western medieval art of illuminating manuscripts, practiced by western monks in both the Early and Late Middle Ages.

Imperial Christianity

As writers, the Byzantines were fond of histories, particularly those detailing the glory days of the old Roman Empire. Even more popular were religious writings that tackled complex questions of theology or described the lives of Christian saints.

The design of the Church of Santa Sophia in Constantinople combined the typical Roman cross-shaped basilica and the dome popular in many Middle Eastern buildings.

The enthusiasm for theological works reflected the value all Byzantines placed on religion. Although the Christian church was important in the west, it was central to the Byzantine Empire. Religion ruled every part of Byzantine life. Brinton notes, "At every important moment in the life of every person, the Church played a . . . role, governing marriage, and family relations, filling leisure time, helping to determine any critical decision. . . . The most serious intellectual problems . . . were those of theology."[35] A great deal of time and energy was spent in religious discussion and argument among all classes of people, from the aristocracy to the working poor. Religious disputes sometimes erupted into destructive riots that lasted for days.

Restoring the Empire

Religion was one of the motives that drove Emperor Justinian I to order the invasion of Italy in 535. The ruling Ostrogoths practiced a form of Christianity known as Arianism, of which neither the Church of Rome nor the eastern church approved. Justinian wished to suppress the Goths' Arianism, which he saw as a heresy.

Justinian, of course, was also motivated by a desire to return Italy, the heartland of the old Roman Empire, to direct imperial rule. Indeed, Justinian wished to reconquer all the lands that had been under Roman control. Although he failed in that goal, the empire did reach its greatest extent under his rule. Justinian's generals not only drove the Goths out of Italy but also took North Africa from the Vandals and the southern part of Spain from the Visigoths.

Justinian's Code

In addition to reclaiming the old territories, Justinian was interested in reforming Byzantine law. The imperial legal code that

Two men pray in this illustration. Religion was at the heart of Byzantine society, affecting every aspect of daily life.

Justinian inherited when he became emperor in 527 was a mixture of the civic laws of Rome, the individual laws of each imperial region, rulings by judges, and imperial decrees. The collection of laws was so confusing that no one understood it. Justinian wanted to end this confusion and to produce a unified, official legal code. He wrote:

> We [Justinian] have found the entire arrangement of the law which has come down to us from the foundation of the City of Rome . . . to be so confused that it is . . . not within the grasp of human capacity. . . . We have hastened to attempt the most complete and thorough amendment [correction] of the entire law, to collect and revise the whole body of Roman jurisprudence [law], and to assemble in one book the scattered treatises [writings] of so many authors.[36]

Justinian's new legal code was rooted in two concepts. First, all law comes from the emperor, and, second, all law must be based on orthodox (that is, officially accepted) Christianity.

The Code of Justinian was in many ways a blueprint of Byzantine society. It ruled that citizens, those born free, were either persons of rank or commoners. It recognized slavery, and although it encouraged the freeing of slaves, it allowed desperately poor parents to sell newborn chil-

This illustration shows the court of the emperor Justinian. One of Justinian's greatest accomplishments was the reform of the Byzantine law code.

The *Secret History* of Procopius

In his published writings the historian Procopius wrote glowingly of Justinian I, whom the scholar knew personally. However, in his Secret History, *unpublished during his lifetime and quoted here from* The Eagle, the Crescent, and the Cross, *edited by Charles T. Davis, he painted a far darker portrait of the emperor. To this day, historians are uncertain which account is more accurate.*

This Emperor . . . was deceitful, devious, . . . cruel, . . . never moved to tears by either joy or pain, though he could summon them . . . at will when the occasion demanded, a liar always, . . . in writing, and when he swore sacred oaths to his subjects in their very hearing. Then he would immediately break his agreements and his pledges. . . . A faithless friend, he was a treacherous enemy, insane for murder and plunder, . . . easily led to anything evil, but never willing to listen to good counsel, quick to plan mischief and carry it out, but finding even the hearing of anything good distasteful. . . .

Nature seemed to have taken the wickedness of all other men combined and planted it in this man's soul. . . . He was too prone to listen to accusations; and too quick to punish. . . . Without hesitation, he wrote decrees for the plundering of countries, sacking of cities, and slavery of whole nations, for no cause whatever.

dren into slavery. Further, even though the Byzantines did not practice feudalism, the code created a class of serfs by ordering that any farmer who remained on his land for more than thirty years had to stay there permanently, as did his children.

Still, the code also provided some protection of individual rights, particularly for women. Under Justinian's laws, a woman could inherit property. Additionally, although divorce by mutual consent was not part of the code until after Justinian's death, a wife could divorce her husband if he were unfaithful, if he accused her falsely of adultery, or if he kept her captive.

Justinian's Legacy

The code was Justinian's most important legacy and his longest lasting, as it remained in effect until the Byzantine Empire ended in the fifteenth century. Justinian left other legacies as well, but these spelled trouble for the Byzantines. Upon the emperor's death in 565, the imperial treasury that had been full when Justinian became emperor was empty because of the costs of his foreign wars. To pay for the governing of the conquered lands, taxes were high, made even higher by corrupt tax collectors.

Justinian's conquests cost the empire more than just money. Because the Byzantines had to shift soldiers to Africa, Italy, and Spain, they weakened their eastern border defenses. Taking advantage of this weakness, the Persian Empire attacked and grabbed off large chunks of the Byzantine state, including Egypt. For a time the empire appeared doomed.

Victory and Defeat

In 610, when Byzantine fortunes were at their lowest, Heraclius, son of the governor of Africa, seized the imperial throne. It took the new emperor ten hard years to rebuild the army and the treasury. Then Heraclius defeated the Persians and regained all the lost territory.

However, Heraclius's victory was costly. Both the Byzantines and the Persians were drained by the years of war, and they were easy marks for Muslim armies that burst out of Arabia in 634. As the Arabs swept over the Middle East and then across Africa and into Spain, Persia fell to them, as did much of the Byzantine Empire. By the middle of the eighth century, almost all of the empire's land outside of Asia Minor and Greece was gone.

Iconoclasts

Military action by the Arabs ended in the early eighth century only to be replaced by a new internal crisis when Iconoclasm, a religious movement, swept the empire. Supporters of Iconoclasm (which means "the breaking of images") claimed that holy statues and painted images, or icons, of the Virgin Mary, Christ, and the various saints were sinful. Such icons were common in Byzantine churches, monasteries, shops, and homes. The Iconoclasts were particularly upset because people seemed to worship the icons, a practice that smacked of the classical religions of Rome and Greece. The image breakers also pointed to

Iconoclasts, who believed images of religious figures were sinful, destroyed paintings and statues of the Virgin Mary, Christ, and the saints.

A Western Visitor in Constantinople

The following account by Bishop Liudprand from northern Italy describes a visit to the court of Emperor Constantine VII in 950 and is reprinted in The Eagle, the Crescent, and the Cross, *edited by Charles T. Davis.*

Before the emperor's seat stood a tree, made of bronze gilded over, whose branches were filled with birds, also made of gilded bronze, which uttered different cries, each according to its varying species. The throne itself was . . . of immense size and was guarded by lions, made either of bronze or of wood covered over with gold, who beat the ground with their tails and gave a dreadful roar with open mouth and quivering tongue. . . .

The emperor . . . invited me to dinner with him. . . . The emperor and his guests . . . recline on couches: and everything is served in vessels, not of silver, but of gold. . . . The solid food fruit is brought on in . . . golden bowls, which are too heavy for men to lift. . . . Through openings in the ceiling hang three ropes . . . with golden rings. These rings are attached to the handles . . . [of] the bowls, and with four or five men helping from below, they [the bowls] are swung on to the table.

the second commandment: "Thou shalt not make unto thee any graven images."

In 726 Emperor Leo III became an Iconoclast and forbade the use and display of icons. Riots exploded as soldiers removing icons were attacked by angry citizens. The next two emperors were also Iconoclasts. Constantine V, Leo's son, was particularly passionate and had thousands of icons destroyed and their owners tortured, mutilated, and killed. Iconoclasm was finally outlawed in 843.

The New Glory

A period of internal and external peace followed the end of the Iconoclasm dispute. The empire, although still the largest and wealthiest in Europe, seemed to have passed its prime and to be in decline. Then, in the last half of the ninth century, a new line of emperors, the Macedonians, came to power and quickly won back some of the land that had been lost to the Arabs. Under the able leadership of the Macedonian emperors, the Byzantine state was once more made strong, and Constantinople had more trade, more wealth, and more art than Rome at its height.

Still, most of the former Byzantine imperial provinces in the Middle East, North Africa, and Spain remained firmly in Muslim hands. In these areas a culture as rich and as sophisticated as the Byzantine Empire arose.

Chapter Six

Islam

In the first decades of the seventh century a new religion arose in Arabia. Called Islam (Arabic for "to surrender to the will of God"), its founder was a former trader and merchant named Muhammad, and its followers were known as Muslims (Arabic for "those who submit"). The early history of Islam was one of the struggle and persecution in its homeland, followed by a final acceptance of Muhammad's teachings and the carrying of the religion to neighboring states by conquering armies.

During the Early Middle Ages contact between Muslims and European Christians was frequently violent, as in the Muslim's conquest of Spain and their on-again, off-again war with the Byzantine Empire. However, Islamic culture was no more warlike than other societies of the time, and the civilization that grew in the Muslim world rivaled—and in some ways surpassed—that of the Byzantines.

Muhammad

Born in the Arabian trading city of Mecca around 570, Muhammad became a trader before marrying a wealthy widow. After his marriage Muhammad had the time and the money to pursue his growing interest in religion, and he began learning more about various religions, probably Christianity and Judaism.

Muhammad often spent nights alone, meditating in a nearby mountain cave. On one such night in 610 he had a vision of the angel Gabriel:

> Whilst I [Muhammad] was asleep, with a coverlet of silk brocade whereon was some writing, the angel Gabriel appeared to me and said,

This illustration depicts Muhammad (whose face has been erased as a sign of respect) and Moses conversing with Gabriel.

صلوة وفي اليوم والليلة وصيام تلك الشهر في كل سنة فقا

لى موسى ان امتك ضعيف لا يطيقون ذلك فارجع الى رب

انت وجبريل و سئله التخفيف لامتك قال النبي عليه السلا

"Read!" I said, "I do not read. . . . " He said, "Read!" . . . So I read aloud, and he departed from me at last. And I awoke. . . . I went forth until. . . . I heard a voice from heaven saying, "O Mohammed thou art the messenger of Allah [God] and I am Gabriel." I raised my head toward heaven to see, and lo, [there was] Gabriel in the form of a man.[37]

Muhammad was at first frightened by his experience but eventually concluded that he had been chosen by God to explain divine will. He immediately began preaching, explaining this and other revelations that came to him in visions.

The Prophet

The Arabs to whom he preached had a number of gods. They also worshipped sacred stones. The most important of these stones, the Black Stone, was in Mecca in the Kaaba (Arabic for "cubic building"), along with several idols. The Black Stone, an oval some seven inches (18cm) in diameter, was said to have fallen from heaven and was probably a meteorite.

Muhammad's teachings called for rejection of these Arabic gods and belief in a single God, who was the same as that worshipped by Jews and Christians. Indeed, Muhammad pointed to the Old Testament prophet Abraham as the founder of Islam as well as of Judaism and Christianity. Muhammad felt that the beliefs of both Judaism and Christianity were generally true but that both earlier religions were incomplete. It was his visions from God that contained the final truth.

Muhammad's preaching was not accepted in Mecca, so in 622 he went to another Arabian city, Yathrib, which became the center for the new religion and which would soon change its name to al-Medinah al-Muhawwarah, meaning "the most glorious city" because of its role in the development of Islam. Muhammad's move to al-Medinah (called Medina in English) became known as the Hegira (Arabic for "flight"), and the year 622 became year 1 of the Muslim calendar.

Medina, however, was not to be the capital of Islam. Muhammad's visions revealed that the Kaaba in Mecca had been built by Abraham, and Muhammad therefore commanded his followers to face toward Mecca and the Kaaba when praying. Because of the importance of Mecca, Muhammad could not allow it to remain in the hands of the old Arabic religion, and in 630 he and his followers attacked and took the city. The idols in the Kaaba were destroyed, although the Black Stone was kept and became an important holy object for Muslims. By the time of Muhammad's death in 632, a third of all Arabs had accepted Islam.

The Beliefs of Islam

After Muhammad's death, Islam began to take a more formal shape. Muhammad's teachings were collected in a book called the Koran, sometimes spelled Qur'an (Arabic for "reading" or "discussion"). Over the centuries a whole body of writings arose to explain the meanings of the book's sections.

Muslims pray in the desert. Muhammad preached that Muslims must pray to a single god every day.

The Constitution of Medina

In 622 Muhammad established a religious government in Medina and set down rules of conduct for Muslims. This order, known as the Constitution of Medina and here quoted from Medieval Europe, *edited by C. Warren Hollister, was the first official document of Islam.*

In the name of God the Compassionate, the Merciful. . . . The God-fearing believers shall be against the rebellious or him who seeks to spread injustice, or sin, . . . or corruption between believers; the hand of every man shall be against him even if he be a son of one of them. . . . Believers are friends one to the other to the exclusion of outsiders. To the Jew who follows us belong help and equality. He shall not be wronged nor shall his enemies be aided. . . . The God-fearing believers enjoy the best and most upright guidance. . . . Whoever is convicted of killing a believer without good reason shall be subject to retaliation unless the next of kin is satisfied with [blood money]. . . .

It shall not be lawful to a believer who holds by what is in this document and believes in God and the last day to help an evil-doer . . . or to shelter him. . . . Whenever you differ about a matter it must be referred to God and to Muhammud. . . .

God approves of this document. This deed [writing] will not protect the unjust and the sinner. The man who goes forth to fight and the man who stays at home . . . is safe unless he had been unjust and sinned. God is the protector of the good and God-fearing man and Muhammud is the prophet of God.

Basic to the belief of all Muslims are the five duties, or the Pillars of Islam. The first duty is to confirm one's faith by saying publicly that "There is no god but God, and Muhammad is his messenger." The second duty requires five daily prayers said while facing in the direction of the Kaaba in Mecca. The third duty is to give alms—charitable donations—to the poor. The fourth is to fast from sunrise to sunset each day of the holy month of Ramadan. The final duty of the Muslim is to make a pilgrimage to the Kaaba in Mecca.

Jihad

Beginning in 634 and continuing throughout the seventh, eighth, and first half of the ninth centuries, these beliefs were brought to many non-Arab lands by Muslim conquerors. The object of the conquerors was to expose as many people as possible to Islam and to persuade them to accept it as their religion.

The Arabs called such a holy war a jihad (Arabic for "battle"). Despite its military definition, a jihad's stated purpose is not to grab territory or to force nonbelievers to convert. Rather, it is to seize political power in order to reach Islam's goal of changing the earth.

Like most human undertakings, however, jihads were not always driven by ideals. Sometimes, the conquerors were more interested in carving out domains to rule than in promoting Islam. Also, jihads opened up conquered lands to large numbers of Arab immigrants. By leaving the Arabian peninsula, these immigrants relieved the overpopulation that had plagued their homeland since the sixth century. Even before the jihad, the strained resources of the Arabian desert had forced many Arabs to move into neighboring Syria, Iraq, and Palestine.

Attacking the Byzantines

Whatever the motives behind them, the jihads of the Early Middle Ages were very

Islamic warriors battle in this illustration. Muslim armies conquered peoples in many non-Arab lands in the seventh, eighth, and ninth centuries.

successful. The Byzantine Empire, the first European state to feel the impact of Islamic jihad in 634, lost Egypt, Syria, and Palestine, including Jerusalem, within five years to the Arabs.

Several factors contributed to the Arab victory, as they would in the Arab takeover of North Africa in 698. First, the Muslim troops were more disciplined and better led than those of the Byzantines. Second, the Byzantine Empire had been drained by years of fighting the Persian Empire and lacked the human and material resources to fight such a determined enemy.

Peoples of the Book

Finally, the Byzantine emperor Heraclius, having recently reclaimed Egypt and Syria for his empire, had cracked down on Jews and on Christian heretics, who made up the bulk of the population of these imperial provinces. As a result, these two groups welcomed the arrival of the Arabs as an escape from Heraclius's policies because the Arabs did not oppress Jews and Christians. Since the latter two groups also believed in a single God, they were, like Muslims, "peoples of the Book," although they followed the Bible and not the Koran.

The Arabs' broad-mindedness did serve Muslim self-interest. Historian Norman F. Cantor writes that Islamic states placed a "tax and limitation of political rights on those who did not recognize Mohammed as the Prophet of Allah, and therefore they

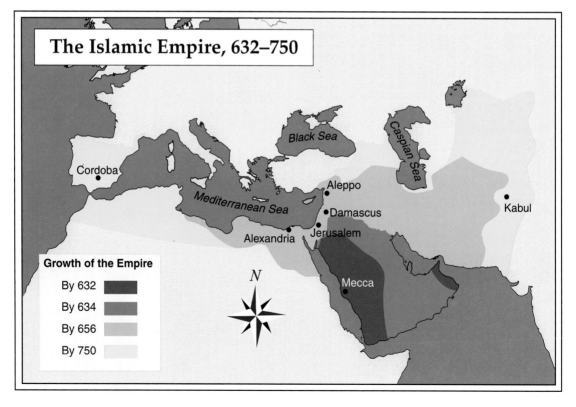

The Islamic Empire, 632–750

Black Sea

Caspian Sea

Cordoba

Mediterranean Sea

Aleppo

Damascus

Kabul

Alexandria

Jerusalem

Growth of the Empire

By 632

By 634

By 656

By 750

N

Mecca

The Conquest of Spain

The ninth-century Egyptian Ibn Abd-el-Hakem relates many stories, some fact and some fiction, about the Muslim campaign in Spain in his History of the Conquest of Spain, *found in* The Eagle, the Crescent, and the Cross, *edited by Charles T. Davis.*

Tarik [leader of the Muslims], . . . having passed by an island, . . . left behind . . . a division of his troops. . . . The Moslems . . . found . . . there . . . vinedressers [grape growers]. . . . They took one of the vinedressers, . . . cut him in pieces, and boiled him. . . . They had also boiled [other] meat. . . . When the meat was cooked, they threw away the flesh of the man; . . . no one knowing that it was thrown away: and they ate the meat. . . . [The vinedressers] . . . informed the people of Andalus [Spain] that the Moslems feed on human flesh. . . .

There was a house in Andalus, the door of which was secured with padlocks, and on which every new king of the country placed a padlock, . . . until . . . the king against whom the Moslems marched . . . refused saying, I will place nothing, . . . until I know what is inside; . . . inside were portraits of the Arabs, and a letter, . . . "When this door shall be opened, these people will invade this country." . . .

When Tarik landed soldiers from Cordova [a Spanish city] came to meet him; and seeing the small number of his companions they despised him. . . . The battle with Tarik was severe. They [the Spanish soldiers] were routed. . . . When [King] Roderic heard of this, he came to their rescue. . . . They [the Muslims and the Spanish] fought a severe battle; but God, mighty and great, killed Roderic and his companions.

had a vested interest in not hurrying the conversion of their subjects."[38]

Victory and Defeat

In addition to the Byzantine Empire, the Visigothic kingdom of Spain became a target for jihad when a Muslim army from Tangiers invaded it in 714. The Visigoths were nowhere near as well organized, trained, or disciplined as their opponents, and their kingdom was soon overrun and conquered.

Other Muslim victories in Europe followed. In 827 Arabs occupied Sicily and other Mediterranean islands. Ten years later, Sicily was used as a base from which to land troops in southern Italy. The Muslims then threatened Rome and the papacy for the next century.

Despite their impressive victories, the Muslims were not unbeatable. Though they tried twice to take the city of Constantinople, thus opening up a route into eastern Europe, they failed both times.

Another northward thrust, this time from Spain, was stopped at Tours by the Franks in 732.

Sunnis and Shiites

To those they fought, the followers of Islam seemed to function with a single mind. In fact, however, Muslims were split into two rival factions—the Sunnis and the Shiites—who struggled for control of the religion's leadership.

After the death of Muhammad, the new Islamic state was ruled by a single leader, known as the caliph. In 656 this post became the prize in a civil war between the Sunnis and the Shiites. The Sunnis desired to elect any Muslim capable of handling the job of caliph, while the Shiites wanted the position reserved for a member of Muhammad's family. The Sunnis also believed that the Koran required additional writings to make its teachings clear, while the Shiites felt that the book needed no explanations, that its lessons should stand on their own.

The Muslim civil war resulted in a shattering of Islamic unity. Each Islamic state was dominated by one or the other faction. Thus, for example, Egypt was under Shiite rule, while Spain was governed by Sunnis. Generally, as Cantor notes, "the rulers of these states continued to respect the caliph as the successor of the Prophet, but the political power in the Islamic world had now fallen into the hand of various . . . princes."[39]

Meanwhile, the caliphate passed first through Sunni hands and then into Shiite hands. The latter moved the caliphate to Baghdad, then a Shiite stronghold.

Islamic Culture

In both Sunni and Shiite states, Arab leaders ruled over a culture that, except for the Byzantine Empire, was far more advanced than Europe was during the Early Middle Ages. The scholar Philip K. Hitie observes that "while [the caliphs] . . . were . . . [reading] Greek and Persian philosophy . . . Charlemagne and his lords . . . were . . . dabbling in the art of writing their names."[40]

Philosophy was an important part of Muslim intellectual life, particularly natural philosophy, or science. Astronomy, for instance, was of such interest that the ninth-century caliph al-Mamun built observatories and had the works of ancient Greek astronomers translated into Arabic. Islamic scientists excelled in chemistry, introducing, historian Will Durant writes, "precise observation, controlled experiment, and careful records. They . . . chemically analyzed . . . substances, . . . studied and manufactured hundreds of drugs."[41] Muslims also excelled at medicine, their medical books providing the most accurate and thorough descriptions of the symptoms and course of smallpox, measles, and eye diseases to be found until the eighteenth century. Muslim doctors even had to pass tests in order to practice.

In addition to science, Muslims did much important work in mathematics, producing significant advances in algebra (an Arabic word meaning "the reduction"). Their only European rivals in mathematics were the Byzantines, who were limited because they used a clumsy numbering system. Like the ancient Greeks, the Byzantines used letters from the Greek alphabet as digits, a practice that made complex calculations difficult. Unlike the Byzantines, Islamic mathematicians had the concept of zero and the easily manipulated Arabic numerals, both of which Arab traders had brought from India.

Education

This vibrant Islamic civilization had many roots. It was the result in part of cultural gains that came with the conquest of Egypt and Persia, homes of very old civilizations. It also developed from the sharing of ideas between people brought together from all parts of the Muslim world by the pilgrimage to Mecca. Further, reading was encouraged because it was a necessary skill in order to study the Koran. Finally, the Muslim culture may have benefited from a tradition that said that Muhammad had urged his followers to learn, saying that "he who leaves his home in search of knowledge walks in the path of God."[42]

To provide access to this path of knowledge, education was available to poor and rich alike. Even non-Muslims could study at Islamic schools, and it was in the universities of Cordova in Spain that westerners found Arabic translations of Greek works, such as those of Aristotle, no longer available in the west. According to one anonymous

Muslim astronomers study the skies in this fifteenth-century illustration. Medieval Muslim scholars were far more advanced in science and mathematics than their European counterparts.

writer of the period, western Europeans were equally enthusiastic about original Muslim writing: "My fellow Christians delight in the poems and romances of the Arabs; they study the works of Moslem . . . philosophers. . . . The young Christians . . .

Medical Guide

Muslim medicine was considerably closer to the modern notion of health care than anything else found in Europe during the Early Middle Ages, as the following passage from a tenth-century manual for doctors reveals (reprinted in Medieval Europe, *edited by C. Warren Hollister).*

Since the science of medicine is very vast and the life of man too short to reach its end, therefore expert physicians . . . busy themselves constantly with the study of books and pore over them by night and day. . . .

Just as you must read all the books written on the practice of medicine, so too must you know the relevant principles of natural science, of which medicine is a branch. You must also be proficient in the methods of logic so that you may . . . refute the fools who pass as physicians. . . .

If you carry out your treatment effectively with diet . . . then do not use drugs, for most of them are enemies . . . of nature. . . .

There is a foolishness widespread among the common people. They regard themselves as physicians for certain ailments. . . . There are notions about medicine which they regard as true and right, though they are clearly false. . . . They . . . believe that . . . the sneeze is the end of the disease.

The medieval Muslim view of health care was remarkably similar to modern ideas. A Muslim physician consults with a patient in this scene from a fifteenth-century manuscript.

read and study Arabic books with avidity, they amass whole libraries of them at immense cost, and they everywhere sing the praises of Arabic lore."[43]

The Development of Europe

These European scholars slowly introduced this lore to the rest of their fellows. Indeed, in numerous ways, Muslim culture would play a major role in the development of European civilization. For example, over the next few centuries westerners took from Muslim Spain architectural features such as pointed arches and the stone patterning called arabesque that became common in European buildings of the Late Middle Ages. Muslims also gave the west the tambourine, the guitar, and the lute. Finally, Islamic science and mathematics would be important to the development of western science that began in the Renaissance.

Despite these eventual contributions to western civilization, Muslim culture had little impact on western Europe during the Early Middle Ages. The west was still too fragmented and politically unstable to profit from its sophisticated neighbors. Indeed, during the final two centuries of the Early Middle Ages, western European societies were fighting for their very existence as they faced the threat of a new group of barbarians—the Vikings.

Chapter Seven

The Vikings

During the ninth and tenth centuries the Vikings, fierce warriors from the Scandinavian north, attacked, killed, and looted as they launched raid after raid against western Europe. These Vikings, also known as Northmen, even attacked Constantinople, the capital of the Byzantine Empire. Yet they were more than just raiders, for they were also explorers, traders, and settlers. In these roles, they colonized Iceland, established powerful states in Britain and Normandy, and founded a trade empire in Russia.

The Norse

The Vikings came from a people known as the Norse, who were descended from German tribes who had moved into the region of Denmark, Norway, and Sweden. As in other German peoples, a warrior elite ruled the Norse. These Norse warriors impressed all who met them, as they did the tenth-century Muslim traveler Ibn Fadlan:

Never had I seen a people of more perfect physique. . . . They wear neither coat nor kaftan [robe], but each man carried a cape which covers one half of his body, leaving one hand free. No one is ever parted from his axe, sword, and knife. Their swords are Frankish in design, broad, flat, and fluted [grooved]. Each man has a number of trees, figures, and the like [tattooed] from the finger-nails to the neck.[44]

The families of these warriors were large because many Norse men had more than one wife. These large families created a problem. The more sons each family had, the less each son received for his inheritance when the father's estate was divided among all his male heirs. This male overpopulation may have caused some Norse warriors to become Vikings in order to increase their wealth. Others became Vikings because they had been exiled from their northern homes, while many were simply drawn by adventure.

Viking Raids

The first Viking raids were small affairs, involving only a handful of ships. The raiders attacked a coastal village or monastery and then returned home with some loot and a few slaves. However, in time, the Vikings began assembling fleets of ships so they could mount attacks against larger and richer targets, such as London or Paris.

The Vikings' ships gave them an advantage in the type of hit-and-run raids they liked. These ships were more advanced than any others to be found in the Early Middle Ages or even at the height of the Roman Empire. Small and powered by both sails and oars, Viking ships were very manageable and could readily sail up rivers, such as the Thames in Britain. Historian David Nicholas remarks that "the geography of northwestern Europe, laced with streams that were easily navigable by the small Viking keels, . . . made the region an easy prey for naval attacks."[45]

This woodcut shows Vikings preparing for a raid. During the ninth and tenth centuries Vikings thrived as explorers, traders, and settlers.

The Vikings' water approach gave their victims little or no warning. In raids from the sea the Northmen sailed right up to a beach, whereas in river attacks they sailed to the mouth of a river and then quickly rowed upstream to reach their goal. Once the Vikings reached the shore, they swarmed out of their ships, generally meeting little resistance, and took what they wanted. The raid finished, the Vikings shoved off and were long gone before land forces, slowed by bad roads—or no roads at all—could reach them. Other ships were rarely a threat to them.

The Viking Reputation

The Vikings were frightening to those they attacked. The northerners seemed without fear and also without pity or mercy. They were savage in their raids, killing, looting,

The Vikings' compact, easily maneuverable ships gave them a great advantage in raids and conquest.

Vikings at Paris

In an eyewitness account, excerpted in A Source Book of Medieval History, *edited by Frederic Austin Ogg, the Frankish monk Abbo describes the massive effort by the Vikings to take Paris in 885.*

The Northmen came to Paris with 700 sailing ships . . . [and] approached the tower [protecting the city] and attacked it. . . . The city resounded with clamor, the people were aroused. . . . All came together to defend the tower. . . . There perished many a Frank. . . . At last the enemy withdrew. . . . Once more the [Vikings] . . . engaged with Christians in violent combat. On every side arrows sped and blood flowed. With the arrows mingled the stones hurled by slings and war-machines. . . . The tower . . . groaned with the struggle, the people ran hither and thither, the bells jangled. The warriors rushed together to defend the tottering tower. . . . Among these warriors, . . . a count, . . . surpassed all the rest in courage. . . . [This count was] Odo who never experienced defeat and continually revived the spirits of the worn-out defenders. He ran along the ramparts and hurled back the enemy. . . .

Meanwhile Paris was suffering not only from the sword outside but also from a pestilence [disease] within. . . . Within the walls, there was not ground enough . . . to bury the dead.

burning, and leaving little behind them. Further, they were not Christians, so they did not hesitate to loot and burn churches and monasteries, killing priests and monks. To Christian Europe, Vikings seemed like devils released from hell.

Records from the time of the attacks note the regular appearance of the northern raiders with the same fatalism as the coming of winter. A nameless ninth-century Frankish chronicler wrote, "the heathen from the North wrought havoc in Christendom as usual and grew greater in strength."[46]

These Viking raids had a major effect on western European life. They strengthened the feudal system at the expense of central authority. In response to the onslaughts, local warlords built castles and fortresses where people could hide safely during a Viking raid. Thus, because they could offer safety to attacked villagers, the lords of these castles became more important to the people than any king or emperor who was too far away to be of help.

Britain and the Danelaw

One of the first targets of the Vikings was Britain, with the first attack being recorded in 787. The raiders were from Denmark, as were most of the other Vikings to attack

Vikings invade Britain in this illustration. Raids like this were so commonplace that medieval Europeans considered them as inevitable as the changing of the seasons.

the British isles. In 865 the Danes established settlements in the center of Britain. From these permanent bases they mounted constant attacks against kingdoms in southern Britain, and within ten years only the kingdom of Wessex was still free of their control.

In 871 Ethelred, the king of Wessex, was killed fighting the Danes and was succeeded by Alfred, his younger brother. Seven years and two defeats later, Alfred finally beat the northerners in battle. He was not strong enough to force the Danes out of Britain, but he was able to draw new boundary lines between his kingdom and their holdings. Thus, Alfred ruled over southern and west central Britain, while the Danes had the north, running up to Scotland, and the east central regions. This Danish section became known as the

Danelaw. Because of his victory, the Wessex king became known as Alfred the Great.

The Danes, who converted to Christianity as part of their deal with Alfred, did not entirely keep within the Danelaw, and periodic fights broke out between them and Wessex. At the beginning of the eleventh century the Scandinavians managed to get one of their own, Canute, on the Wessex throne. Canute ruled over a kingdom comprising Britain, Denmark, and Norway. This state, though, lasted only a few years, as upon Canute's death the Wessex throne went to another native Briton.

Vikings and Normans

In 841, some fifty years after the raids on Britain started, the Vikings began striking hard at the western Franks. In 885 a huge fleet of seven hundred Viking ships sailed up the Seine and attacked Paris. When they could not take the city outright, the Northmen set up a siege that lasted two years and ended only after the Frankish ruler Charles the Fat paid them a large sum of money and allowed them to plunder part of his kingdom.

As they had in Britain, the Vikings built permanent bases, this time on the northwestern coast of the Frankish kingdom. The Franks began calling these Northmen Normans and the Norman-occupied region became known as Normandy.

In 911 the Frankish king Charles the Simple made a deal with the Viking chief Rollo. If Rollo and the other Normans stopped raiding and converted to Christianity, Charles would make Rollo duke of Normandy. Rollo accepted the offer, and the duchy of Normandy, one of the great powers of the Late Middle Ages, was born. The Normans went on to conquer England and to form Norman states in Sicily, southern Italy, and the Middle East.

The Rus

The Vikings also raided closer to home along the Baltic coastline, where they eventually established bases. Setting out from these bases at the end of the eighth century, bands of Swedish Vikings made long raiding expeditions into what is now Russia. In order to protect themselves from the local inhabitants, the raiders set up forts along their route, the largest being Novgorod. The Vikings finally reached and took over the town of Kiev, where they became known as the Rus (Finnish for "Swede"), from which comes the name Russia.

In the ninth century the native Slavs drove the Rus back to the Baltic. However, the Slavs soon fell to fighting among themselves, and in the 850s, according to the anonymous twelfth-century *Russian Primary Chronicle,* decided to call the Rus back:

> There was no law amongst them [the Slavs], but tribe rose against tribe. Discord . . . ensued among them, and they . . . began to war against one another. They said to themselves "Let us seek a prince who may rule over us according to the law." They accordingly went overseas . . . and said to the people of Rus, "Our whole land is great and rich, but there is no

Viking chief Rollo (standing) leads an attack. Rollo became duke of Normandy after he agreed to stop raiding the Franks and converted to Christianity.

order in it. Come to rule and reign over us."[47]

A Viking called Rurik used this plea as an excuse to take over Novgorod. Oleg, Rurik's successor, expanded the Rus holdings to once again include Kiev.

In 907 Oleg, with two thousand ships and eighty thousand men, attacked Constantinople. The Vikings posed such a threat to the city that the Byzantines agreed to a trade treaty with the Rus on Oleg's terms. This treaty turned Kiev into a major trade center. With a route that stretched from Constantinople to the Frankish kingdom, the Rus of Kiev linked eastern and western Europe. From the east came jewelry, silk, furs, spices, and silver; from the west, wine, wheat, wool clothing, swords, and metal tools. The wealth from this trade would fuel the expansion of the Kiev state, which would transform into the Russian empire in the Late Middle Ages.

Viking Explorers

The Vikings were always looking for new lands to conquer, and so, in the ninth century, they turned their attention away from Europe toward the unknown Atlantic. Their seventh-century invention of the keel gave them ships that could handle even the rough waters of the North Atlantic.

The Viking Duke

In 911, as described in the eleventh-century Chronicle of St. Denys Based on Dudo and William of Jumieges, *quoted in* A Source Book of Medieval History, *edited by Frederic Austin Ogg, Charles the Simple, the king of the West Franks, made the Viking Rollo duke of Normandy in order to stop Viking looting of his kingdom.*

The king had at first wished to give Rollo the province of Flanders, but the Norman [Viking] rejected it as being too marshy. Rollo refused to kiss the foot of Charles when he received . . . the duchy of Normandy. . . . "Never," replied he, "will I bend the knee to any one, or kiss anybody's foot." . . . King Charles, . . . the counts, . . . and the bishops and abbots, bound themselves by the oath . . . to Rollo, swearing by their lives and by their bodies and by the honor of all the kingdom, that he might hold the land and transmit it to his heirs. . . .

Rollo gave assurance of security to all those who wished to dwell in his country. The land he divided among his followers. . . . It was peopled by the Norman warriors and by immigrants from outside regions. The duke established for his subjects . . . rights and laws. . . . He rebuilt the churches, . . . which had been destroyed by the [Vikings]; . . . he repaired the walls . . . of the cities.

In specially designed ocean-going vessels, Viking explorers discovered Iceland in 825, settling it almost fifty years later in 872. Other Viking ships moved west, discovering and settling Greenland. In about 992, according to tradition, Vikings under the command of Leif Eriksson reached North America, which the seafarers called Vinland. Unlike the Icelandic colony, however, all the other Viking settlements died out and were forgotten.

Iceland

In the tenth century Iceland saw a surge in population as thousands of settlers arrived from Norway. These colonists were seeking to free themselves from the Norwegian king, who they felt held too much of the political power in the state. The attraction for them was that Iceland had no ruler. Instead, the island was governed through the Althing, an assembly of landholders that met once a year. The Althing passed laws by majority vote, but it had to depend on the willingness of Icelanders to obey these laws since the assembly had no power of enforcement.

As a consequence, no central authority existed to stop the many deadly feuds that broke out between upper-class Icelandic families. Nicholas observes that "Iceland was an exceptionally violent place, where the blood feud lived on. The freedom enjoyed by the population testifies . . . to the unwillingness of anyone to accept subordination to [the authority of] the community."[48]

Despite this ongoing violence, Iceland became a cultural storehouse over the centuries. Icelanders composed poetry and fictional narratives, such as the *Elder Edda* and the *Volsunga Saga*, that provided details of the Norse religion and way of life, as well as recording Viking deeds, such as Leif Eriksson's voyage to North America. The most famous of the Icelandic writers was Snorri Sturluson. Among his works are the *Prose Edda*, which tells the story of the Norse gods, and the *Heims Kringla*, a history of the Kings of Norway.

The Last of the Vikings

The settling of Iceland was the last Viking adventure, for the end of the tenth century marked the end of the Viking era. In part, the end came because of changes in Scandinavia. Kingdoms had arisen in Denmark, Norway, and Sweden, and Norse aristocrats turned their talents to running these new realms instead of going raiding. Further, Christianity spread through Scandinavia and replaced the old Norse religion. The new religion, unlike the old, did not promote the Vikings' warrior values, which consequently died out.

In part, the end arrived for the Vikings when they became permanent inhabitants of Britain, Normandy, Russia, and other parts of Europe. In these foreign lands the Vikings and their culture disappeared into that of the surrounding society. Thus, the Danes became Britons and the Normans Franks.

Yet there always remained reminders of the Viking past. English personal pronouns, for instance, are Scandinavian in origin, as are the words *brook, hill,* and *grove.* Normandy is filled with towns whose names derive from Norse first names, such as Quetterville, whose founder was the Viking Ketril.

The End of an Era

With the disappearance of the Vikings, western Europe was finally free of the threat of outside invasion and large-scale attack for the first time in five centuries. Without such threats, western European civilization would finally have the opportunity to mature. This civilization would contain elements from its Germanic, Roman, and Viking past and would incorporate much from its neighbors in the Byzantine and Muslim empires. It was a culture whose foundation was laid

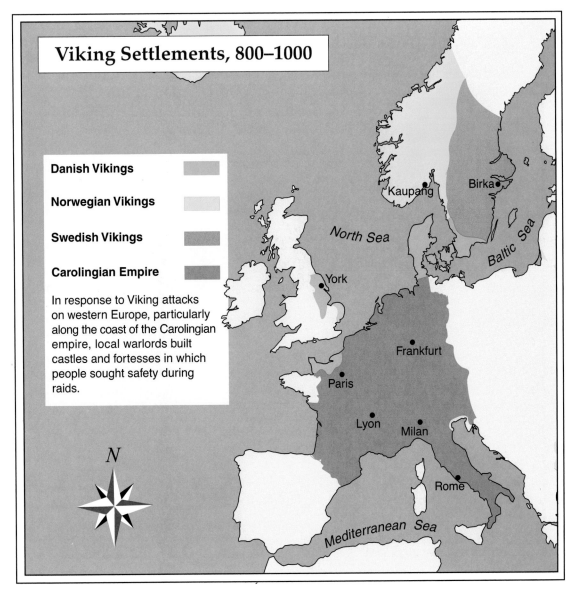

Viking Settlements, 800–1000

Danish Vikings

Norwegian Vikings

Swedish Vikings

Carolingian Empire

In response to Viking attacks on western Europe, particularly along the coast of the Carolingian empire, local warlords built castles and fortesses in which people sought safety during raids.

Kaupang

Birka

North Sea

Baltic Sea

York

Frankfurt

Paris

Lyon

Milan

Rome

Mediterranean Sea

N

Leif Eriksson Visits Vinland

Around 992, as related in the thirteenth-century Greenlanders Saga, *found in* Medieval Europe, *edited by C. Warren Hollister, Leif Eriksson landed on the North American coast, probably in present-day Labrador. He then pushed farther south, eventually reaching either Nova Scotia or New England, which he called Vinland (Wine Land) because of its grapes.*

At the first landfall they . . . lowered a boat and landed. There was no grass to be seen, and . . . [the ground] was covered with great glaciers, and between glaciers and shore the land was like one great slab of rock. . . .

Leif said, . . . "I shall . . . [call] this country . . . *Helluland* [Hell's Land]."

They returned to the ship and put to sea, and sighted a second land. . . . This country was flat and wooded, with white sandy beaches. . . . Leif said, "This country shall be . . . called *Markland* [Wood Land]."

They hurried back to their ship . . . and sailed away . . . until they sighted land again. . . .

They went ashore. . . . The weather was fine. There was dew on the grass, and the first thing they did was to get some of it on their hands and put it to their lips, and to them it seemed the sweetest thing they had ever tasted. . . .

Leif said to his men, . . . "On alternate days we must gather grapes . . . and then fell trees, to make a cargo for my ship." . . . Leif named the country after its natural qualities . . . *Vinland.*

This statue of Leif Eriksson stands in Reykjavik, Iceland. Although Viking explorers including Eriksson reached North America, they did not establish permanent settlements there.

Although Viking culture eventually died out, reminders such as this Viking cemetery in Jutland, Denmark, still exist.

in the five centuries of the Early Middle Ages. As historian Archibald R. Lewis observes:

> The eleventh century dawned on a new European civilization. . . . This new Europe was a blend of diverse traditions, peoples, and cultures. . . . This new Europe . . . was no sudden affair, but a slow process, covering a number of centuries, in which each . . . Barbarian, Merovingian, Carolingian, Viking . . . played a . . . role. . . . The story of Europe during this period [the Early Middle Ages] is not one of a dark age followed by a sudden recovery, but of a developing civilization.[49]

Notes

Introduction: The Beginnings of a New Civilization

1. C. Warren Hollister, *Medieval Europe: A Short History.* Boston: McGraw-Hill, 1998, p. 1.
2. Quoted in James Westfall Thompson, *The Middle Ages, 300–1500.* New York: Cooper Square, 1972, p. xii.
3. Justine Davis Randers-Pehrson, *Barbarians and Romans: The Birth Struggle of Europe, A.D. 400–700.* Norman: University of Oklahoma Press, 1983, p. 3.
4. Archibald R. Lewis, *Emerging Medieval Europe, A.D. 400–1000.* New York: Knopf, 1967, p. xi.

Chapter 1: The Barbarians

5. David Nicholas, *The Evolution of the Medieval World: Society, Government and Thought in Europe, 312–1500.* London: Longman, 1992, p. 17.
6. Quoted in Jonathan F. Scott, Albert Hyma, and Arthur H. Noyes, eds., *Readings in Medieval History.* New York: Crofts, 1933, pp. 24–25.
7. Crane Brinton, John B. Christopher, and Robert Lee Wolff, *A History of Civilization.* Vol. 1, *Prehistory to 1715.* 2nd ed. Englewood Cliffs, NJ: Prentice Hall, 1960, p. 177.
8. Quoted in Will Durant, *The Story of Civilization.* Vol. 4, *The Age of Faith.* New York: Simon and Schuster, 1950, p. 39.

9. Quoted in Brian Tierney, ed., *The Middle Ages.* Vol. 1, *Sources of Medieval History.* 3rd ed. New York: Knopf, 1978, p. 46.

Chapter 2: The Church

10. Norman F. Cantor, *The Civilization of the Middle Ages.* New York: Harper-Collins, 1993, p. 146.
11. Ralph H.C. Davis, *A History of Medieval Europe: From Constantine to St. Louis.* 2nd ed. London: Longman, 1988, p. 78.
12. Davis, *History of Medieval Europe,* p. 78.
13. Nicholas, *Evolution of the Medieval World,* p. 73.
14. R. Allen Brown, *The Origins of Modern Europe: The Medieval Heritage of Western Civilization.* Woodbridge, UK: Boydell, 1972, p. 85.
15. Hollister, *Medieval Europe,* p. 69.
16. Hollister, *Medieval Europe,* p. 69.
17. David Knowles and Dimitri Obolensky, *The Christian Centuries.* Vol. 2, *The Middle Ages.* New York: McGraw-Hill, 1968, p. 155.

Chapter 3: The Franks

18. Quoted in Brinton, Christopher, and Wolff, *History of Civilization,* pp. 182–83.
19. Cantor, *Civilization of the Middle Ages,* p. 189.

20. Durant, *Story of Civilization*, p. 484.
21. Cantor, *Civilization of the Middle Ages*, p. 172.
22. Quoted in Brian Pullan, ed., *Sources for the History of Medieval Europe, from the Mid-Eighth to the Mid-Thirteenth Century.* Corrected ed. Oxford: Blackwell, 1971, p. 38.
23. Nicholas, *Evolution of the Medieval World*, p. 120.

Chapter 4: Feudalism

24. Brinton, Christopher, and Wolff, *History of Civilization*, p. 196.
25. François L. Ganshof, *Feudalism*. Trans. Philip Grierson. 3rd ed. Toronto: University of Toronto Press, 1996, p. 22.
26. Quoted in C. Warren Hollister, Joe W. Leedom, Marc A. Meyer, and David Spear, eds., *Medieval Europe: A Short Sourcebook.* 3rd ed. New York: McGraw-Hill, 1997, p. 107.
27. Quoted in Ganshof, *Feudalism*, p. 33
28. Nicholas, *Evolution of the Medieval World*, p. 162.
29. Ganshof, *Feudalism*, p. 19.
30. Quoted in Scott, Hyma, and Noyes, *Readings in Medieval History*, pp. 197–98.

Chapter 5: The Byzantines

31. Nicholas, *Evolution of the Medieval World*, p. 82.
32. Nicholas, *Evolution of the Medieval World*, p. 91.
33. Brinton, Christopher, and Wolff, *History of Civilization*, p. 213.
34. Quoted in Brinton, Christopher, and Wolff, *A History of Civilization*, p. 216.
35. Brinton, Christopher, and Wolff, *History of Civilization*, pp. 227–28.
36. Quoted in Charles T. Davis, ed., *The Eagle, the Crescent, and the Cross: Sources of Medieval History, Volume I (c. 250–c. 1000).* New York: Appleton-Century-Crofts, 1967, p. 115.

Chapter 6: Islam

37. Quoted in Durant, *Story of Civilization*, pp. 163–64.
38. Cantor, *Civilization of the Middle Ages*, p. 133.
39. Cantor, *Civilization of the Middle Ages*, p. 137.
40. Quoted in Nicholas, *Evolution of the Medieval World*, p. 111.
41. Durant, *Story of Civilization*, p. 244.
42. Quoted in Durant, *Story of Civilization*, p. 234.
43. Quoted in Brinton, Christopher, and Wolff, *History of Civilization*, p. 255.

Chapter 7: The Vikings

44. Quoted in Davis, *The Eagle, the Crescent, and the Cross*, pp. 154–55.
45. Nicholas, *Evolution of the Medieval World*, p. 138.
46. Quoted in Frederic Austin Ogg, ed., *A Source Book of Medieval History.* New York: Cooper Square, 1907, p. 161.
47. Quoted in Brinton, Christopher, and Wolff, *History of Civilization*, p. 242.
48. Nicholas, *Evolution of the Medieval World*, p. 137.
49. Lewis, *Emerging Medieval Europe*, pp. 165–67.

For Further Reading

Books

James Barter, *The Late Middle Ages*. San Diego: Lucent, 2005. This history completes the story of the Middle Ages and is filled with instructive illustrations. It contains excerpts from period documents, maps, a time line, and a reading list.

———, *Life in a Medieval Village*. San Diego: Lucent, 2003. Filled with reproductions of period woodcuts, paintings, and drawings, this volume describes the daily lives and activities of medieval villagers.

Thomas Bulfinch, *Bulfinch's Mythology*. New York: Modern Library, 1998. This classic contains a lively retelling of the medieval legends that grew up around Charlemagne. The introduction gives useful information about the background of the tales.

Phyllis Corzine, *The Islamic Empire*. San Diego: Lucent, 2004. This book traces the history of the Islamic world from its beginning through the twelfth century. It relies on both period and scholarly writings to examine the literary, artistic, and scientific achievements of Islamic society.

Ruth Dean and Melissa Thomson, *Women of the Middle Ages*. San Diego: Lucent, 2002. This informative book details the lives of medieval women: peasants, healers, estate managers, queens, religious women, writers, and artists.

Miriam Greenblatt, *Charlemagne and the Early Middle Ages*. New York: Benchmark, 2002. This biography of Charlemagne also examines aspects of Frankish society such as education and religion. It quotes from Frankish poems, letters, laws, and diaries and has many full-color reproductions of period art.

Allison Lassieur, *The Vikings*. San Diego: Lucent, 2001. Relying largely on archaeological evidence, this title tells the story of the Vikings and their impact on Europe.

Bruno Leone, ed., *The Middle Ages*. San Diego: Greenhaven, 2002. With sources ranging from religious tracts to eyewitness testimony of historical events, this collection provides insight into the social and personal affairs of the time.

Donald Matthew, *Atlas of Medieval Europe*. New York: Facts On File, 1992. This volume is filled with large, easily read maps in color of Early Middle Ages places and artifacts. A good commentary with special sections on such topics as the Carolingian renaissance and the Christian church is supported by a time line and a bibliography arranged by country and topic.

Don Nardo, *The Byzantine Empire*. San Diego: Blackbirch, 2005. This book describes everyday life in the Byzantine Empire from that of the emperor to farmworkers.

———, *The Fall of the Roman Empire*. San Diego: Lucent, 2004. This study explores the reasons for the decline and fall of Rome over the course of three centuries and includes a detailed look at the barbarian invasions.

Victoria Sherrow, *Life in a Medieval Monastery*. San Diego: Lucent, 2000. Using both period and scholarly sources, this work examines life inside the medieval monastery.

Thomas Streissguth, *Greenhaven Encyclopedia of the Middle Ages*. San Diego: Greenhaven, 2003. This one-volume reference offers broad coverage of the people, events, and philosophies of the Middle Ages. Over 500 entries are followed by an appendix that lists rulers, leaders, and popes. A time line and bibliography of both primary and secondary works round out the text.

Web Sites

Internet Medieval Sourcebook (www. fordham.edu/halsall/sbook.htm). This site links to many Early Middle Ages documents, most of which are modern translations.

The Net's Educational Resource Center (members.aol.com/teachernet). This useful site provides links to Early Middle Ages overviews, terms, maps, time lines, daily life, culture, and beliefs.

Teacher Oz's Kingdom of History (www. teacheroz.com). This excellent site has hundreds of links to Early Middle Ages images and subjects such as feudalism, Vikings, religion, warfare, and biographies.

Works Consulted

Books

Crane Brinton, John B. Christopher, and Robert Lee Wolff, *A History of Civilization*. Vol. 1, *Prehistory to 1715*. 2nd ed. Englewood Cliffs, NJ: Prentice Hall, 1960. The chapters on the Early Middle Ages give a good, clear outline, as well as presenting a balanced account, of the period.

R. Allen Brown, *The Origins of Modern Europe: The Medieval Heritage of Western Civilization*. Woodbridge, UK: Boydell, 1972. The chapters on the Early Middle Ages discuss the cultural evolution of European society during this period.

Norman F. Cantor, *The Civilization of the Middle Ages*. New York: HarperCollins, 1993. This thorough history of the Middle Ages by an eminent medieval scholar provides facts and insights into the people and events of the Early Middle Ages. It also contains a useful reading list and a list of recommended films about the Middle Ages.

Charles T. Davis, ed., *The Eagle, the Crescent, and the Cross: Sources of Medieval History, Volume I (c. 250–c. 1000)*. New York: Appleton-Century-Crofts, 1967. This collection is an excellent source of Early Middle Ages writing. Each piece is either by or about a major figure from the period.

Ralph H.C. Davis, *A History of Medieval Europe: From Constantine to St. Louis*. 2nd ed. London: Longman, 1988. This short study tells the history of the Middle Ages concisely and clearly.

Will Durant, *The Story of Civilization*. Vol. 4, *The Age of Faith*. New York: Simon and Schuster, 1950. This classic study of the Middle Ages is written in a readable, accessible style and ends with a large bibliography. Its chapters on the Early Middle Ages are filled with facts, incidents, and speculation about the time.

François L. Ganshof, *Feudalism*. Trans. Philip Grierson. 3rd ed. Toronto: University of Toronto Press, 1996. This excellent study presents a history of the development of feudalism and a description of how the feudal system operated.

C. Warren Hollister, *Medieval Europe: A Short History*. Boston: McGraw-Hill, 1998. The first section of this book by a famous medieval scholar is a good, short history of the Early Middle Ages.

C. Warren Hollister, Joe W. Leedom, Marc A. Meyer, and David Spear, eds., *Medieval Europe: A Short Sourcebook*. 3rd ed. New York: McGraw-Hill, 1997. This useful volume contains many original writings from the Early Middle Ages, most of which are modern translations.

David Knowles and Dimitri Obolensky, *The Christian Centuries*. Vol. 2, *The Mid-*

dle Ages. New York: McGraw-Hill, 1968. This thorough, scholarly history of both the western and eastern Christian church in the Early Middle Ages has a valuable time line of events, a listing of popes, and many photographs of medieval church buildings and art.

Archibald R. Lewis, *Emerging Medieval Europe, A.D. 400–1000.* New York: Knopf, 1967. This good, short history of the Early Middle Ages looks at both western and eastern Europe and emphasizes the social changes of the period.

David Nicholas, *The Evolution of the Medieval World: Society, Government and Thought in Europe, 312–1500.* London: Longman, 1992. This sound study shows how religion, politics, art, and everyday life contributed to the development of the Middle Ages from the fall of Rome to the Renaissance. Each chapter ends with a list of suggested readings, and the book has an excellent map section at the back.

Frederic Austin Ogg, ed., *A Source Book of Medieval History.* New York: Cooper Square, 1907. This collection is one of the best sources for original writings from the Early Middle Ages. Lengthy excerpts from period documents have thoughtful introductions explaining the importance of each selection.

Brian Pullan, ed., *Sources for the History of Medieval Europe, from the Mid-Eighth to the Mid-Thirteenth Century.* Corrected ed. Oxford: Blackwell, 1971. The editor presents a varied selection of original Early Middle Ages writings, newly translated for this book.

Justine Davis Randers-Pehrson, *Barbarians and Romans: The Birth Struggle of Europe, A.D. 400–700.* Norman: University of Oklahoma Press, 1983. This extensive study details the major German tribes and the kingdoms that each established at the beginning of the Early Middle Ages.

Jonathan F. Scott, Albert Hyma, and Arthur H. Noyes, eds., *Readings in Medieval History.* New York: Crofts, 1933. This volume is a classic source of original writings from the Early Middle Ages, particularly useful for material about the medieval church and feudalism.

James Westfall Thompson, *The Middle Ages, 300–1500.* New York: Cooper Square, 1972. This one-volume history of the Middle Ages provides much useful information on the Early Middle Ages.

Brian Tierney, ed., *The Middle Ages.* Vol. 1, *Sources of Medieval History.* 3rd ed. New York: Knopf, 1978. This book is a useful, short collection of original writing from the Early Middle Ages.

Index

Stephen II (pope), 42
Sturluson, Snorri, 96
Sunnis, 84
suzerain. *See* lords

Tacitus, 16–17
Theodohad (king of the Ostrogoths), 26
Theodoric the Great (king of the Ostro-
goths), 24–25
trade, 68–69, 95
Treaty of Verdun, 49

Vandals, 21, 23, 71
vassals
duties and responsibilities of, 54–55
honorable service by, 55–56
immunity of, 61, 63

manor of, 58, 59–60
multiple oaths made by, 62
power of, 57
relationship between lords and, 53–54
Vikings
descendants of, 88–89
exploration by, 95–96, 98
invasions by, 10–11, 91
legacy of, 96–97
raids of, 89–93, 95, 97
Viollet, M. Paul, 13
Virgil, 38
Visigoths, 10, 19–21, 33, 47, 83

women, 56–57, 69, 73

Zeno (Byzantine emperor), 24

Picture Credits

About the Author

James A. Corrick has been a professional writer and editor for twenty-five years. Along with a PhD in English, his academic background includes a graduate degree in the biological sciences. He has taught English, edited magazines for the National Space Society, and edited and indexed books on history, economics, and literature. Corrick and his wife live in Tucson, Arizona. Among his other titles for Lucent are *The Renaissance, The Industrial Revolution, The Civil War: Life Among the Soldiers and Cavalry, The Louisiana Purchase, Life of a Medieval Knight, The Inca, The Civil War,* and *Life Among the Inca.*